2·50

GUEST OF THE SOUL

GUEST OF THE SOUL

BY
COMMISSIONER S. L. BRENGLE, D.D., O.F.

THE SALVATION ARMY
SUPPLIES AND PURCHASING DEPT.
Atlanta, Georgia

GUEST OF THE SOUL

First published in 1934

Reprinted 1982

ISBN: 0-86544-001-8

Printed in the United States of America

PREFACE

IT is with exceptional pleasure that, on the eve of my retirement from the position of General of The Salvation Army, I welcome the publication of another book by our veteran Holiness Apostle, Commissioner Brengle, whose writings for many years have spread blessing far beyond the confines of The Army.

This small volume contains some of the gems of the Commissioner's thought and experience. All but one of the papers have been written in the author's ripe old age; and in his spirit the " seventy summers " to which he refers in his Birthday retrospect are truly far more evident than the " seventy winters."

These choice contributions to the growing treasury of Salvation Army literature will be valued in all parts of the world. They will, I am sure, serve to strengthen the faith of the readers of this book, and impress upon them the joyousness of life when the heart has been opened to the Holy Guest of the Soul.

Those tens of thousands who during the past year have read and been stirred by the splendid biography of the Commissioner—

who, fortunately, is still with us—will particularly appreciate the reproduction in this volume of the notable address on " The Atonement," repeatedly mentioned in the life-story. Here, indeed, is rich food for thought. I am sure that at the end of this study of the mystery of our Lord's sacrifice of love many a reader will bow his head in adoration and exclaim : My Lord and my God !

We all thank Commissioner Brengle for this book, and with him I trust that it will lead to the saving and sanctifying of many souls.

EDWARD J. HIGGINS.

London,
    October, 1934.

CONTENTS

I. THE ATONEMENT

NOTE

IT was my joyful privilege in the early part of 1907 to spend five months in intensive and fruitful evangelistic work in Norway. Two extreme movements were attracting wide attention in the country. In Oslo, then known as Christiania, what is popularly known as " The Tongues Movement " was arousing unusual interest—as indeed it was throughout Norway and in other parts of Northern Europe. It was claimed that the apostolic gifts of the Spirit were restored to the Church, and many were seeking the baptism of the Holy Spirit—with special emphasis placed upon the gift of Tongues, as the one necessary and invariable sign of the baptism.

In Bergen, the second city of the kingdom, the so-called " New Theology " had been accepted and preached with eloquence and zeal by one of the most popular and influential State clergymen in the city. Other pastors flew to the defence of the faith in learned arguments, which left the man in the street in much perplexity and uncertainty. Since I was to visit Bergen, the local Salvation Army officer, Adjutant Theodor Westergaard,* wrote begging me to speak on the subject, promising to secure the finest hall in the city (the one in which the

* Now Colonel, in charge of Salvation Army work in Finland.

controversy had begun and been carried on) and to gather a representative audience to hear me.

I have never considered myself so much an advocate as a witness, and I did not wish to begin a few days' revival campaign by getting mixed up in a controversy of which I knew so little, and with a gentleman of whom I knew nothing. However, I wrote the Adjutant that, if he wished to advertise me to speak on the Atonement from the standpoint of an evangelist and a witness, he might do so. I was then visiting the cities on the south and west coasts of Norway ; conducting two, three and four meetings a day ; travelling, poor sailor that I am, on little, comfortless coastal steamers, with no books but my Bible and Song Book, and no one with whom I could talk over the subject ; with almost every waking hour filled with work, wearied with long and exacting meetings. I could make only a few notes on an envelope I carried in my pocket. But I prayed, meditated, communed with God, sought His inspiration and guidance, thought my way through my subject, and trusted for Divine help.

The following is in substance the address of that evening in Bergen,* clothed in the language used as nearly as I was able to recall after some weeks in which I was still engaged in exacting labours. It is in no sense an exhaustive study of the Atonement. I was in a strange city on the eve of only a few days of evangelistic labours

* For a detailed description of the meeting, which proved historic, see Clarence W. Hall's *Samuel L. Brengle,* pp. 237–241.

for the salvation of sinners and sanctification of believers. The object of the address was not so much to answer critics and to satisfy the demand of scholarship, as to reach the hearts of men—of plain men and women—with the importance, the need, the nature of God's great gift of love and sacrifice in His Son for the redemption of men.

I had but one hour, and had to speak through an interpreter, who took up half my time. There was no opportunity for elaborate reasoning or for the discussion of various theories of the Atonement; I was able to give just a simple presentation of truth that would win men to Christ and reconcile them to God. During the following eight days' meetings more than six hundred men, women and children publicly sought pardon and purity.

S. L. BRENGLE.

* * *

NO other subject the human mind can consider is so vitally important, so humbling, and yet so ennobling in its effect, as the Atonement, the work and act of our Lord Jesus Christ in suffering and dying for men that He might save them from sin.

It is a subject which leads to the profoundest questions and oftentimes to the most perplexing and distressing doubts, which cannot be ended by argument, nor settled by human learning and skilful reason-

ing, but only by faith in the records found
in the Bible and wrought out in experience.
Nevertheless, arguments and illustrations
may in some measure help our faith and
guide our minds to a right understanding
of a matter which is either of infinite importance or else of no importance at all.

SIN : WHAT IT IS

Right in the forefront of the discussion
we are face to face with the great problem
of sin. If there is no sin, no evil estrange-
ment from God, then there is no need of an
Atonement, of a Divine sacrifice to save us.

What is sin ? Is it only a mild infirmity
due to the immature development of the
race, which will be outgrown and corrected
by age, like many of the faults and ignor-
ances of children; or is it a malignantly
wrong attitude of the will and affections
which will never correct itself? Is it a
moral disease which, like measles and
whooping cough, we need not seriously
fear, and to which we may indeed safely
expose our children ; or is it like a hopeless
leprosy or cancer, for which there is no
known cure ? I once stepped off the train
at home and was met with the announcement
that my boy had the measles. I was not
alarmed, and he soon recovered. But later
I visited a leper hospital, and, oh ! the

horror of it! There were hopeless invalids
with their eyes eaten out and their hands
and feet eaten away by the awful disease,
looking longingly for death to come and
give them release. There was no human
cure for them.

If sin is something that corresponds not
to measles, but to leprosy, I can understand
how God, if He loves us and is truly
interested in us, might make some great
sacrifice, some Divine interposition to save
us. And it is this sacrifice, this interposition, which constitutes the Atonement.

But *is* sin like leprosy—an awful moral
corruption, a malignant attitude of the will
and the affections, a corruption of the moral
nature that corresponds to leprosy? The
Bible says it is. But do the Bible and human
history and human experience agree?

In our sheltered Christian homes, and
under the protection of laws framed in the
light of twenty Christian centuries, we are
apt to forget or entirely overlook the
malignant character of sin. People brought
up in homes where the Bible is read and
hymns are sung; where the Ten Commandments are upheld; where a blessing is asked
upon the food, and prayers are offered
morning and evening—such good people
have little conception of the wilful devilry
into which men and women sink, and they

are liable to be led by their own respectability into a false conception of sin.

SIN : AN ACT

What is sin ? God says, " Thou shalt not kill ! " Is it sin to kill ? An intelligent woman accidentally poisoned a baby in her home. Was it sin ? No one who knew her considered it so. It was an awful mistake, and not a sin ; for her will and affections were not malignant, and she was one of the chief mourners at the funeral of the baby.

A little five-year-old child was the first-born pet and darling of its parents ; but then another little one was born into the household, and some foolish women— wickedly foolish women—came into that home and said to the little five-year-old, " You are not Mama's baby and darling now. Mama has another baby that she loves." Jealousy was kindled in that little heart, and one day the child came to its mother with blood on its little hands and said, " Now I am Mama's baby, and now Mama will love her darling "; and Mama flew to the infant, only to find its head battered in with a hammer by the little five-year-old. That was sin—baby sin— but *sin* !

Bear with me while we take a glimpse into the dark depths of what God sees, at what grieves and provokes Him, at some symptoms and manifestations of this hateful thing called sin, which stirred His heart of infinite love and pity and holiness to make such sacrifice to save sinners.

At the height of Rome's power and civilization the emperor murdered his mother, stamped the life out of his wife and unborn child, and lighted the streets of the city with Christians, whom he had covered with pitch and set on fire. That is *sin*—sin full-grown. That is not spiritual measles ; it is moral and spiritual leprosy.

When I was in Switzerland they told me of a man and woman who threw their new-born child, born out of wedlock, to the pigs. That was *sin* !

Why are we shocked at the bare recital of such a story ? It was a common thing at the height of Greek and Roman civiliza-tion to expose children to beasts, and they were expected to destroy the weak baby.

Do you say we have outgrown this ? Why has not China outgrown it ? A lady missionary from China told me that she asked a Chinese mother whether she had ever killed one of her girl babies. The woman replied, " Yes, several of them." And when the missionary asked how she could find it in her heart to do such a brutal thing, the woman laughed. It is still

common in China. One of our Salvation
Army officers rescued a deserted baby left
to be devoured by dogs. It is not that we
have outgrown China, but we have been
lifted out of that terrible darkness and
brutality by Pierced Hands. It is the light
of the Cross shining upon us that has made
the approval of such deeds impossible
amongst us.

SIN: A STATE OF HEART

But sin is not merely an act. It is a state
of the heart as well. A professing Christian
said to me, " There is pride in my heart,
and I get angry "; and I tried to draw a
word picture which would show her the
sin of pride and anger.

" Here is Jesus in Pilate's judgment hall.
They have spat in His face, and crowned
Him with thorns, and stripped Him, and
tied His hands to His feet, and beaten His
bare back till it is bruised and bleeding.
And they have placed the cross upon His
shoulders; and, pale and worn with the
bitter agony, with the spittle on His face,
and the blood on His brow, He struggles up
the hill under the heavy load.

" You come behind Him, and you say,
' I am His follower. I am a Christian. I love
Him.' He is the very essence of lowliness
and humility, but you come strutting behind

Him in pride—proud of the feather in your hat ; of the bloom on your cheek ; of your money in the bank ; of your home, better than other people have ; of your good name ; or of some gift that lifts you above others. You are proud of these things, look down with a certain superciliousness and condescension on others, and consider yourself just a little bit better than they, and hold yourself aloof from them, while professing to follow this lowly Cross-Bearer. You have a right to be grateful to Him for those gifts which have lifted you above others, but no right to be proud, and your pride is an abomination and sin before Him, a spiritual leprosy which only God can heal.

" But He has reached the top of the hill. Hard, rough soldiers have thrown Him down upon the cross, and driven the nails through His hands and feet, and, lifting the cross, have set it in its socket with a terrible thud, adding agony to the suffering Victim. And they mock Him, and rob Him of His only suit of clothes, and cast dice for His seamless robe ; and He prays, ' Father, forgive them ; for they know not what they do ! '

" And you stand at the foot of the Cross, a professing Christian, His follower ; and some man or woman approaches you, and you frown and step aside, for you are angry with that one. In the presence of that compassionate and forgiving Sufferer on the Cross I say that your anger is a sin, which cannot be washed out with rose-water. It is moral leprosy. It is a malignant thing, which cannot be washed out with a few tears, but must be purged with blood, the blood of God's dear Son."

SIN : A CRIME AGAINST GOD

But sin is a crime against God. If I murder a man, I sin against him, and his poor wife, and his helpless children. But they do not punish me; the State punishes me. I have sinned against the State and the whole community. I have broken its laws. I have made a breach in the safeguards which secure the people from crime and danger, and that breach can be closed only by my punishment.

Looking at it in this light, we can rise to the vision of sin as a blow against God and His righteous government, and the safeguards He has thrown around His moral creation. David stole the wife of Uriah the Hittite and secured the murder of Uriah, but, when self-convicted by the story of the prophet Nathan, he saw that he had sinned against God, and cried out, "Against Thee, Thee only, have I sinned, and done this evil in Thy sight" (Psalm li. 4).

Hundreds of years before, Joseph had

been tempted to commit a similar sin. He resisted and overcame the temptation, saying, " How then can I do this great wickedness, and sin against God?" (Gen. xxxix. 9).

How could these men say that this sin, which in such a peculiar sense is a sin against man, was sin against God? Listen! Do you remember the parable of Jesus describing the final Judgment?

Then shall the King say unto them on His right hand, Come, ye blessed of My Father, inherit the kingdom prepared for you from the foundation of the world : for I was an hungred, and ye gave Me meat : I was thirsty, and ye gave Me drink : I was a stranger, and ye took Me in : naked, and ye clothed Me : I was sick, and ye visited Me : I was in prison, and ye came unto Me.

Then shall the righteous [with meek and lowly and wondering surprise] answer Him, saying, Lord, when saw we Thee an hungred, and fed Thee? or thirsty, and gave Thee drink? When saw we Thee a stranger, and took Thee in? or naked, and clothed Thee? or when saw we Thee sick, or in prison, and came unto Thee? And the King shall answer and say unto them, Verily I say unto you, Inasmuch as ye have done it unto one of the least of these My brethren, ye have done it unto Me.

Then shall He say also unto them on the left hand, Depart from Me, ye cursed, into everlasting fire, prepared for the devil and his angels :

for I was an hungred, and ye gave Me no meat :
I was thirsty, and ye gave Me no drink : I was
a stranger, and ye took Me not in : naked, and
ye clothed Me not : sick, and in prison, and ye
visited Me not.

Then shall they also answer Him [with wonder
and indignant surprise], saying, Lord, when
saw we Thee an hungred, or athirst, or a
stranger, or naked, or sick, or in prison, and
did not minister unto Thee ? Then shall He
answer them, saying, Verily I say unto you,
Inasmuch as ye did it not to one of the least of
these, ye did it not to Me.

And these shall go away into everlasting
punishment : but the righteous into life eternal
(Matt. xxv. 34–46).

And what meaning has the parable but
this : that the King so identifies Himself
with every needy and suffering subject in
His vast domain that neglect of, or a blow
against, that subject is counted by the King
as a sin against Himself ? It is God's law
that is broken. It is God's authority that is
defied. It is God's holiness and justice that are
despised. When a man sins, it is against God.

Indeed, sin is nothing less than lawless-
ness—a huge selfishness—that amounts to
moral and spiritual anarchy. The sinner
would pull God off His throne and kill
Him if He could. I was not a bad boy as
men count badness, but I can remember
how, in my childish pride and vaulting

ambition, I wondered why I should be a creature subordinated to God and subject to His righteous and unfailing judgments; and I disliked Him and wished I could pull Him off His throne and seat myself upon it, so that I might be responsible to no one but myself. And does not Jesus teach in His parable of the householder that this is the character of sin?

There was a certain householder, which planted a vineyard, and hedged it round about, and digged a winepress in it, and built a tower, and let it out to husbandmen, and went into a far country: and when the time of the fruit drew near, he sent his servants to the husbandmen, that they might receive the fruits of it. And the husbandmen took his servants, and beat one, and killed another, and stoned another.

Again, he sent other servants more than the first: and they did unto them likewise.

But last of all he sent unto them his son, saying, They will reverence my son. But when the husbandmen saw the son, they said among themselves, This is the heir; come, let us kill him, and let us seize on his inheritance. And they caught him, and cast him out of the vineyard, and slew him (Matt. xxi. 33-39).

What does Jesus teach here but that sin is a state of heart rebellion that, carried to its final issues, would rob and kill God Himself if that were possible? Every sinner wants to have his own way, and gratify his own desires and pleasures, regardless of the glory of God and the highest good of men. The sinner in reality wants to be a law unto himself, wants to be his own God.

Sin can fawn and appear innocent and fair to behold, but it is utterly false and cruel. There are men and women, possibly in your street, who would not hesitate an instant to rob you, if they could, of your last penny and leave you a homeless beggar. They would not hesitate a moment to debauch your innocent boy, your lovely daughter, your sweet sister, and sink them to the lowest depths of infamy, and then glory in their shame. How little do we know the awful depths and darkness of sin! the corruption, the iniquities, the wickednesses, the vile affections, the lusts, the vaulting ambitions that sin leads men into! And what will God do with a hateful thing like this? What attitude must God take toward sin?

GOD'S ATTITUDE TOWARD SIN

(1) He cannot be *ignorant* of sin.

(2) He cannot be *indifferent* to sin. It cannot be said of Him, as it was of Gallio, that He " cared for none of those things " (Acts xviii. 17).

(3) He cannot *approve* sin, for then He would be the chief of sinners.

(4) *God must be utterly and totally antagonistic to sin, and that with all the strength of His great moral being.*

He must hate and condemn sin. Frederick W. Robertson, the great Brighton preacher, when he heard of a so-called gentleman plotting the ruin of a beautiful, innocent girl just budding into womanhood, ground his teeth and clinched his fists in hot indignation. If a righteous man feels that way in the presence of sin, how do you think a holy God must feel? If God does not hate sin He is not holy; if He does not condemn sin He is not righteous; if He is not prepared to punish sin He is not just. But God is holy, He is righteous, He is just. His great heart demands, and His holiness calls for, the utter condemnation of sin. But, oh! my brother, while God is holy and hates sin with a perfect hatred, yet God is love; and while His holiness demands the punishment and utter destruction of sin, His great heart of love calls for the salvation of the sinner.

SIN: A PROBLEM FOR GOD

How shall God accomplish this double and seemingly contradictory demand of His holy and loving heart ? How shall God's love and holiness harmonize to secure mercy for the sinner and judgment against the sin ? How can God be just, and yet justify the ungodly ? How can God look upon sin and justify an ungodly man, and yet be a holy God ? If a judge on the bench is careless in the way he deals with criminals, or a magistrate winks at crime, he is a dangerous man ; that judge, that magistrate, is a dangerous character if he does not watch over the interests of society and deal hardly and severely with wrong-doing. And is it not exactly the same with God ? How shall God deal with this matter of sin ? How shall His great heart of love secure its end : the salvation of the sinner, and His great heart of holiness secure its end : the condemnation of sin ? How shall God justify the ungodly, and yet Himself be just ?

Here is a problem for God. Fools mock at sin, but God does not. Foolish men and women think it is a very simple problem, this matter of the forgiveness of sins ; but it is the profoundest problem in the moral universe, one which no other religion save the Christian religion has been able to solve—and in its solution lie our hope and our peace.

A man commits many crimes and adds to

them rebellion and murder, and he is cast into prison. His friends appeal to the ruler to forgive him, and they think it an easy and a simple thing for him to do. But can the ruler do it? He has the authority, but can he do it and be just and safeguard his people? There are many things he must consider:

(1) Would it not harm the man himself to pardon him, if he were not truly repentant?

(2) Would it not encourage evil men in wickedness, and that possibly in far distant parts of the ruler's dominion?

(3) Would it not endanger society and dismay good men, by sweeping away the safeguards of law and order, and by ignoring, if not destroying, the distinction between well-doing and wrong-doing?

God is confronted with a problem like this. How do we know, when we talk lightly about God's mercy, what other worlds are looking on to see how God will deal with sin in this world? Children watch to see how the wrong-doer will be treated, and nothing will encourage them more quickly to walk in evil ways than to see the wrong-doer smiled and fawned upon.

Parents who have several children know how very careful they must be in dealing with a wrong-doer. Their hearts may feel very tender towards the little one who has done wrong, their hearts may be breaking with desire to save him from punishment; but his future and highest good must be placed first, and the other children must not be allowed to think it a light thing to do wrong. There are two ways of ruining children—the way of the harsh father and the way of the indulgent mother. Too much indulgence and too great severity will alike ruin the children. Blessed are the children whose parents know how to keep an even balance between their desire for their children's pleasure and happiness and the necessity of being firm and unbending in the presence of wrong-doing.

To hold an even balance between goodness and severity is Divine. " Behold therefore the goodness and severity of God," says Paul (Rom. xi. 22). God is faced with the same kind of problem as we are. How can He at the same time be merciful and just and yet secure the well-being of all His vast dominions ? If God forgives sin, if He pardons the sinner before he is penitent, He will only do the man harm.

SIN: HOW CAN GOD FORGIVE IT?

How then can God forgive sin and be just?

(1) He must secure a true spirit of repentance in the sinner, else the man whom He forgives will only be hardened in sin.

(2) He must make all wrong-doers to know that they cannot sin with impunity in His vast empire.

(3) He must safeguard all other moral beings. He must make them feel the holiness of the law and the righteousness of His judgments, until they cry out, "Just and true are Thy ways, Thou King of saints . . . Even so, Lord God Almighty, true and righteous are Thy judgments" (Rev. xv. 3; xvi. 7).

How can He do this? I think we can make it plain by a simple illustration. Our own relations with one another—parents with children, and rulers with their subjects —reflect in some measure the relations of God with men, and the problems with which God is confronted in that relationship.

A great teacher, a lover of men and boys, and a profound student of human nature, kept a school, and had under his care a boy who was a ringleader in wrong-doing. The teacher had to punish the boy several times, but the boy broke the rules again and again most flagrantly. One day the boy committed a more than usually grave offence, and was called up for punishment. The punishment was to be two or three sharp raps with a ferrule on his open palm. The boy had been punished before, but seemed to enjoy breaking the rules of the school and causing trouble to the teacher.

The teacher knew that it would not do to allow this to go on. But he was greatly perplexed. He did not want to cast the boy out of the school. He loved the boy, and longed to bless and save him, but how could he make him to see and understand ? How could he let the child go free and at the same time make the other children feel that it was not a slight thing to break the rules of the school ?

He stood there with an aching heart in the presence of the defiant boy, when all at once a happy inspiration came to him. He said something like this to the boy, " I don't wish to punish you, but when law is broken somebody must suffer. It is always so, my boy, not only in school but out of school as well. But instead of punishing you to-day you shall punish me. I will suffer for you."

The boy looked at him and grew crimson. " Give me the punishment," continued the teacher. The boy looked as if he were in a bath of fire. His heart began to melt under a manifestation of love such as he had never witnessed or heard of before. The teacher stretched forth his open hand and said, " Strike ! " After long hesitation the poor little fellow nerved himself and struck one blow. And then his proud, rebellious little heart broke, he burst into penitential tears, and from that day he became " a new creature."

The teacher never had any more trouble with that boy, while the other children felt that it was not a light thing to break the rules of the school. The teacher had found a way to justify a disobedient child, and yet make wrong-doing look hateful in the eyes of every other child. " He himself suffered, the just for the unjust."

An ancient king passed a law against a certain grave crime. The punishment was to be the loss of both eyes. The first criminal discovered was the king's own son. And now what would the king do ? How could he save his son and uphold the law throughout his dominion, and compel his subjects to reverence him and admire his justice ? How could justice and mercy be wedded ? The king had said that two eyes must be put out. Could they not be the eyes of a slave ? If so, his subjects might fear, but not reverence, the king. They would despise him, and the son would go on in his shameless career.

This is what the king did. He put out one of his son's eyes and put out one of his own eyes, and the people could only exclaim, " The king is merciful, and the king is just." He had found a way to save his son, and at the same time to make the law honourable.

THE ATONEMENT

Will God act so? Will God suffer to save the sinner? Is there any other way by which God can justify the sinner, and yet Himself be just? Is there any other way by which God can display His hatred of sin and His pitying love of the sinner? Is there any other way by which God can break the sinner's proud and unbelieving heart and melt it into penitence and contrition? Is there any other way by which God can retain the respect and confidence of unfallen angels when He pardons sinners and treats them as though they had not sinned? Oh, will God suffer for me? Will He take my place, and in His love and pity die in my stead, to save me from my sin and its direful consequences?

The Bible says that God will suffer, and that God has suffered. *This is the Atonement*

—God's act of condescension and mercy, which bridges the gulf between sinful man and the holy God; between a wicked, fallen creature and an offended Creator; between a wilful and defiant child and a wounded and grieved and loving Father.

JESUS CHRIST: WHO IS HE?

But when and where did God suffer for me?

On Calvary!

But was that dying man on Calvary, God?

He was the God-Man, the Son of God, God the Son (John i. 1–14; 1 Tim. iii. 16).

How can we know God, and where can we find Him?

The heaven of heavens cannot contain Him.

We cannot see Him. We cannot by searching find Him, but *He has focussed Himself, as it were, in Jesus Christ.* He has humbled Himself to our flesh and blood, and stooped to take upon Himself our nature (Phil. ii. 5–8; Heb. ii. 14, 16).

The Bible says, " In the beginning was the Word, and the Word was with God, and the Word was God. . . . The Word was made flesh, and dwelt among us, . . . full of grace and truth " (John i. 1, 14). The Bible says He was God.

[31]

The Apostle Paul says, " Feed the church of God, which He hath purchased with His own blood " (Acts 20. 28).

Then that Sufferer hanging there was God, suffering for us—God, the Blessed Son. Wonder of wonders ! Think of Him pouring out His life, an innocent Sufferer for sinful men, for you and me ! " God was in Christ, reconciling the world unto Himself " (2 Cor. v. 19), and " In all their affliction He was afflicted " (Isa. lxiii. 9).

The Father's heart of love was pierced with pain by the thorns that pierced the head of the Son. The Father's heart was hurt with the nails that pierced the hands and feet of the Son. The Father's heart was thrust through with anguish at the guilt and sins of men when they thrust the spear into the heart of Jesus. The Father suffered with and in the Blessed Son.

The whole Trinity is involved in the atoning work of Jesus Christ on Calvary. The Father " so loved the world, that He gave His only begotten Son " (John iii. 16). " He hath made Him to be sin for us, who knew no sin ; that we might be made the righteousness of God in Him " (2 Cor. v. 21). And it was " through the eternal Spirit " that Christ " offered Himself without spot to God " (Heb. ix. 14), in our stead and on our behalf. Blessed be God !

Truly does Paul say : " Without controversy great is the mystery of godliness:
God was manifest in the flesh " (1 Tim.
iii. 16).

The Bible says that Jesus is God. Jesus
says so, John says so, Paul says so. The
Church in all its creeds says so. The wisest
Christian teachers say so. The saints and
martyrs, who have perished by flame and
wild beast's fang, say so. The great soul-
winners say so. The humble penitents,
rejoicing in the assurance of sins forgiven,
say so ; and with commingling tears and
smiles, and heaven-lit faces, they cry out
with Thomas, " My Lord and my God ! "
(John xx. 28).

But the testimonies of the Bible and the
creeds and the martyrs and saints and soul-
winners and rejoicing penitents do not make
me to know that Jesus is Lord, and I may
still doubt. How shall I know ? May I
know ? A man born blind may hear a
thousand testimonies to the beauties of the
starry heavens and the glories of sunrise and
sunset, and yet doubt them all. He knows
only by hearsay. Is there any way to
destroy his doubts forever ? Only one, and
that is to give him his sight. Then he will
doubt no more. He knows. He sees for
himself.

An astronomer writes a booklet announc-

ing the discovery of a new star. I may read
his booklet, and yet may doubt. What shall
I do? Throw his booklet away, and sit
down and write a bigger book than his, to
prove that there is no such star, and that he
is star-mad or a liar? Nay, nay, rather let
me turn my telescope to that point in the
heavens where he says he found the new
star—and lo! I find a star mirrored in my
telescope! But what if I am mistaken?
Then let another man, two men, a thousand
men in different parts of the earth turn their
telescopes to that point in the heavens; and
if they, too, unanimously say, " There is a
star," how can I doubt any longer?

THE INWARD REVELATION

How can we know that Jesus is Lord?
Paul says, "No man can say that Jesus is the
Lord, but by the Holy Ghost" (1 Cor.
xii. 3). The Holy Ghost must reveal Him to
each heart before doubts about His person
can be destroyed. The Bible is the Book on
Divine astronomy that tells when and where
to discover Him, " the bright and morning
star." It does not reveal Him any more
than the book on astronomy reveals the
stars to a man. It is only a record of self-
revelation, and it tells us how to secure a
personal revelation of Him to our own
hearts.

Let us, then, carefully read the instructions in the Bible—the text-book on this heavenly astronomy, look with the eye of faith through the telescope of God's word, and by true repentance and obedient faith put our souls into that attitude which will enable Him to reveal Himself to us. Let us do what He tells us to do without murmuring and complaining, and lo! as myriad others before us have done, we shall find Him formed within our hearts, " the hope of glory." Our doubts will vanish ; our sins shall be forgiven, our guilt be put away; we shall be " born again," born of the Spirit; we shall have our eyes anointed with spiritual eye salve, and have our hearts made pure to see God, and to discover who Jesus is. Then the Atonement, made by the shedding of His blood, will no longer be an offence to our imperfect reason and a stone of stumbling to our unbelief, it will be the supreme evidence of God's wisdom and love to our wondering and adoring hearts.

It was this inward and spiritual revelation of Christ that gave Paul such assurance and power. He says, " I know whom I have believed " (2 Tim. i. 12), and again, " It pleased God . . . to reveal His Son in me " (Gal. i. 15, 16), and yet again, " I live ; yet not I, but Christ liveth in me " (Gal. ii. 20).

Oh! the joy and infinite peace and

satisfaction contained in this spiritual manifestation of Jesus to the heart! It is a fulfilment of those wonderful words of Jesus (John xiv. 16–27): "I will come to you. . . . At that day ye shall know that I am in My Father, and ye in Me, and I in you . . . I will manifest Myself to" you.

I sat beside a student when Christ was manifested to him, and saw his face shining almost like the face of an angel, and heard him whisper, "Blessed Jesus! blessed Jesus!"—and later heard him saying over and yet over again and again, "Glory be to Jesus! Glory be to Jesus!"

I knelt beside a young lady in prayer, when all at once she burst into tears and cried out in an ecstasy, "O Jesus!" He had come, and she knew Him as Lord. Six months later she said, "I'm going to Africa," and with Christ in her heart she went joyfully as a missionary to darkest Africa, where she lived and laboured and loved, until one day He said: "It is enough, come up higher"; and she went to Heaven by way of Africa.

A great business man found Jesus, and with radiant face and deepest reverence he said, "I was so mixed up with Jesus that for several days I hardly knew whether it was Jesus or I."

A timid little boy, who was afraid to be

left alone in the dark, had the great inward revelation and said quietly and joyfully, " I'm not afraid now, for Jesus is with me."

THE GREAT UNVEILING

Who, then, is Jesus Christ ? Listen to Isaiah :

Unto us a child is born, unto us a son is given ; and the government shall be upon His shoulder : and His name shall be called Wonderful, Counseller, The mighty God, The everlasting Father, The Prince of Peace. Of the increase of His government and peace there shall be no end (Isa. ix. 6, 7).

We look into the Bethlehem manger, and we see only a child, a little son ; and we are indifferent, though wise men and angels welcome and worship Him with reverent awe and wonder. But by-and-by, overcome by the insurrection of our passions and tempers and led captive by sin, finding no help in ourselves and proving that " vain is the help of man," we look again, and lo ! we see that He is our help, and that " *the government shall be upon His shoulder*." And repenting with brokenness of heart, and believing on Him, we find pardon and victory and peace as we look ; and when the impurity of our nature is more fully revealed we find instant cleansing in His blood, and sanctification full and free in

His baptism with the Holy Spirit, and we cry out, " *Wonderful !* "

Again, we are filled with perplexity. Life is a labyrinth, the universe is a riddle, we walk in a maze. We are at our wits' end. Wise men and philosophers cannot answer our anxious questions about the mystery of life ; none can solve the problems of triumphant evil and thwarted goodness, of pain and sorrow and loss and death. And again we look, and lo ! we discover that in Him "are hid all the treasures of wisdom and knowledge " (Col. ii. 3). He answers our questions. He resolves our riddles. We rest in Him as our " *Counseller.*"

Again, we are oppressed with our utter littleness and weakness. We feel as helpless as an insect in the presence of the giant forces of the material universe. We are powerless to resist the vast world movements of men, the strikes, the conspiracies, the huge combinations, the wars, the political and social upheavals. And in our horror and despair we look again, and lo ! we see Him in the earthquake and tempest, "towering o'er the wrecks of time," stilling the storm, raising the dead, calming the fierce, wild passions of men, and slowly but surely enlightening and moulding the nations ; and we cry out, " *The mighty God !* "

Again, we are bereft and lonely and

heart-sore. We cry like an orphaned child in the night, and there is none to help, and no one understands. Then He draws nigh with infinite comprehension of our heartache and weariness and pain, and with fathomless consolations He folds us in the embrace of His love; and we pillow our heads and our hearts on His bosom, and nestle close and whisper, "*The everlasting Father! The Prince of Peace!*"

THE ETERNITY OF OUR LORD

Again, we strain our eyes, peering into the future, wondering what its issues will be, and what it holds for us and ours. Our loved ones and friends die, and pass out of our sight. Life weakens, its full tides ebb, the sun is setting, the night is falling, and we stand by a silent, shoreless sea, where we look in vain for a returning sail, and upon which we must launch alone. And we cling to life, and shrink back with fear, and lo! He comes walking on the waters, and says, "It is I. Be not afraid!" And we are comforted with a great assurance that nothing shall separate us from His love, that He is Lord of life and death, of time and eternity, and that "*of the increase of His government and peace there shall be no end.*" Hallelujah!

This is Jesus. We saw Him first a little

Babe, a helpless Child, on the bosom of a
virgin mother, in a stable among the cattle.
But oh! how He has grown as we have
looked! He "inhabiteth eternity" (Isa.
lvii. 15). "The heaven and heaven of
heavens cannot contain" Him (1 Kings
viii. 27). But He stooped to our lowly
condition and humbled Himself, and suffered
and died for us, and made atonement for
our sins.

And "how shall we escape, if we neglect
so great salvation?" (Heb. ii. 3).

Oh, the bitter shame and sorrow,
   That a time could ever be
When I let the Saviour's pity
Plead in vain, and proudly answered:
   "All of self and none of Thee!"

Yet He found me; I beheld Him
   Bleeding on the cursèd tree,
Heard Him pray, "Forgive them, Father,"
And my wistful heart said faintly:
   "Some of self and some of Thee!"

Day by day His tender mercy,
   Healing, helping, full and free,
Sweet and strong, and, ah! so patient,
Brought me lower, while I whispered:
   "Less of self and more of Thee!"

Higher than the highest heavens,
   Deeper than the deepest sea,
Lord, Thy love at last has conquered,
Grant me now my spirit's longing—
   "None of self and all of Thee!"

The Atonement

I once heard General William Booth, Founder of The Salvation Army, in the midst of an impassioned appeal to men to repent and make their peace with God, cry out, " Every sinner must be either pardoned or punished." And, ever since, these words have remained in my memory as the expression of a tremendous truth from which there is no escape.

As I have written elsewhere : *

The Atonement opens wide the door of pardon, of uttermost Salvation, and of bliss eternal to every penitent sinner who will believe on Christ and follow Him, while it sweeps away every excuse from the impenitent sinner who will not trust and obey Him.

The Atonement justifies God in all His ways with sinful men.

The holiest beings in the universe can never feel that God is indifferent to sin, when He pardons a believing sinner, lifts up his drooping head and introduces him to the glories and blessedness of Heaven, because Christ has died for him. On the other hand, the sinner who is lost and banished to outer darkness, cannot blame God nor charge Him with indifference to his misery, since Christ, by tasting death for him, flung wide open the gateway of escape. That he definitely refused to enter in will be clear in his memory for ever, and will leave him without excuse.

* In *Love Slaves*, chapter 3.

" Judas went to his own place."
Now, I ask again—oh ! " *how* shall we
escape, if we neglect so great salvation ? "

Was it for me, for me He died,
  And shall I still reject His plea ?
Mercy refuse with foolish pride,
    The while His heart still yearns for me ?
      Shall I my cup of guilt thus fill,
      While Jesus pleads and loves me still ?

    Dear Saviour, I can ne'er repay
      The debt of love I owe !
    Here, Lord, I give myself away,
      'Tis all that I can do.

II. THE BLESSEDNESS OF THE PENTECOSTAL BAPTISM

If ye then, being evil, know how to give good gifts unto your children : how much more shall your heavenly Father give the Holy Spirit to them that ask Him ? (Luke xi. 13).

Ye shall receive power, after that the Holy Ghost is come upon you (Acts i. 8).

PENTECOST was the first great event in the history of our religion after the Ascension of Jesus. It was the fulfilment of Joel's prophecy and Jesus' promise.

Joel, hundreds of years before, had prophesied :

It shall come to pass afterward, that I will pour out my spirit upon all flesh ; and your sons and your daughters shall prophesy [that is, speak for God], your old men shall dream dreams [of a better day coming than they ever knew], your young men shall see visions [of a world redeemed from sin and conquered for Christ by service, by willing sacrifice, by patient suffering, by endurance to the utmost] : and also upon the servants and upon the handmaids in those days will I pour out my spirit (Joel ii. 28, 29).

And Jesus Himself had promised that if He went away He would send another

Comforter or Helper, who would be with them evermore.

Before He ascended to the Father, He commanded His disciples

that they should not depart from Jerusalem, but wait for the promise of the Father, which, saith He, ye have heard of Me. For John truly baptized with water; but *ye shall be baptized with the Holy Ghost* not many days hence (Acts i. 4, 5).

On the day of Pentecost came the ample fulfilment. They were all filled with the Holy Ghost. That was the final and all-sufficient evidence that Jesus had not been swallowed up and lost in the cloud that had received Him out of their sight, but that He had got Home to Heaven, that He was upon His Throne, and that in His exaltation and exultation He had not forgotten them. They were still in His thought and in His love; He was depending upon them still, and equipping them with power to carry on His work and fulfil His purpose.

They were exultant. Their joy overflowed. They shined and they shouted. Their hearts caught fire, their minds kindled into flame. Their tongues were unloosed. They must testify. They trooped downstairs from the upper room and out into the street. This was no mere drawing-room, parlour-holiness-meeting blessing they had received. It was too big, too glorious and good to be confined. They must tell it abroad.

The city of Jerusalem was full of strangers from all parts of the world, come to the great feast; and to these strangers in their own language the glorious news was told. The populous city was stirred, mystified, and there was a rush together of the curious multitude, and they were "confounded," "amazed." They "marvelled" as every man heard them speak in his own language. In their amazement and doubt they exclaimed, "What meaneth this?"—and well they might. It meant that God had come to tabernacle in the hearts of men, that all Heaven was enlisted in a campaign for the salvation of the world, a campaign which would not cease till the earth was "filled with the knowledge of the glory of the Lord, as the waters cover the sea" (Hab. ii. 14).

But some mocked, and said, "These men are full of new wine," they are drunk; and so they were, drunk with holy joy and gladness and love and quenchless hope and life eternal.

Peter said: "*This* is that which was spoken by the prophet Joel," and so it was. The other Comforter had come, and the great days of the Church were inaugurated with a mighty revival, in the first meeting of which 3,000 people were converted. And every revival from then till now—whether local, in some little church or Salvation Army hall or mission station; or world-wide in its sweep like the Wesleyan revival, or that led by William Booth—has flowed from the presence and activities of the Holy Spirit as He has been received in trusting hearts and honoured in faith and service.

All the lovers of Jesus should in these days seek fresh renewings and a greater fullness of the Holy Spirit. They should study what the Bible says about Him as a Person. He is not a mere influence, passing over us like a wind or warming us like a fire. He is a Person, seeking entrance into our hearts that He may comfort us, instruct us, empower us, guide us, give us heavenly wisdom, and fit us for holy and triumphant service.

If we will seek His presence and yield ourselves to Him in secret prayer, He will make the Bible a new book to us. He will make Jesus precious to us, He will make God the Father ever real to us. We shall not walk in darkness, but shall have the light of life. We shall not be weak in the presence of duty or temptation, but " strong in the Lord, and in the power of His might "

(Eph. vi. 10). We shall be " ready to every good work " (Titus iii. 1).

I suggest to all my readers that by way of preparation they prayerfully and carefully study what Jesus says of the Holy Spirit, " the Comforter," in John xiv, xv, and xvi, and that the Acts of the Apostles, which in many respects might be called the Acts of the Holy Ghost, be read and re-read again and again, and pondered in faith and prayer.

God has greater things for us and all His people than the world has ever yet seen, if we but believe on the Lord Jesus Christ and permit the Spirit to lead us.

As many as are led by the Spirit of God, they are the sons of God. . . . And if children, then heirs ; heirs of God, and joint-heirs with Christ (Rom. viii. 14, 17).

And the heir can draw on the estate for all those things needful for his well-being and the full development and use of his powers.

* * *

The baptism of the Holy Ghost is not given to any and everybody. Jesus spoke of Him as One " whom the world cannot receive, because it seeth Him not, neither knoweth Him " (John xiv. 17). Jesus did not say, " *may* not receive," but " *cannot* receive." He is given only to those who can receive, to those who see and know. If a man has

[47]

closed his eyes to light, if he has turned his heart from true knowledge, he cannot receive. And yet such people are responsible for their deprivation, because their blindness is due to their own action. Such people could not receive the Holy Ghost because *they prepared not their hearts to receive Him.* They turned away from the Saviour and the truth which alone could fit them to receive Him.

The Holy Ghost is given only to those who, accepting Christ and following Him, are prepared to receive. The Pentecostal baptism is for an inner circle. It is a family affair. It is for the children who have become sons and daughters of God through penitent, obedient faith. It is part of their heritage. It is the portion of that immeasurable inheritance in Christ which is bestowed upon them while upon earth. What the measure of that full inheritance will be in the heavenly world no tongue can tell, no heart can conceive. Pentecost is the foretaste. It is that which, received and properly, wisely, diligently used, will fit us for the final and full reward, but which, rejected or neglected, will leave us eternal paupers among those who weep and gnash their teeth in outer darkness.

(1) *The Pentecostal Blessing is for our comfort while we are away from Home and from the unveiled presence of the Father.* " I will not

leave you comfortless," said Jesus, "I will come to you" (John xiv. 18). The coming of the Comforter is also the coming of Jesus in the Spirit. Where the Spirit is there Jesus is. When He is come we are no longer orphans, lonely and bereft. Though unseen He is present with us, and our hearts are strangely warmed and comforted. To some of us this world would be desolate and lonely beyond words if it were not for the presence of the Comforter.

(2) *The Pentecostal Blessing is for our instruction in the things of God.* The Holy Ghost is the great, secret, silent, inward Teacher, speaking to the ears of the soul, whispering in the silences of the night, instructing in the hours of prayer and communion. We are dull and ignorant, making no assured progress in the School of Christ, until the Comforter is come.

But the Comforter, which is the Holy Ghost, whom the Father will send in My name, He shall teach you all things, and bring all things to your remembrance, whatsoever I have said unto you (said Jesus) (John xiv. 26).

When He comes He arouses and quickens our dull minds. He opens wide the closed eyes, the sealed ears of the soul ; and we see and hear things that were hidden from us. He brings our inner life into harmony with

[49]

the mind of God as revealed in the Bible,
and its spiritual meaning begins to open up
to our understanding. He quickens our
memory and we now can remember the
word of the Lord. We can go home from
a meeting and tell what we have heard when
the Comforter is in our hearts.

(3) *The Pentecostal Blessing is for our
guidance.* There is one way that is everlasting. " Lead me in the way everlasting,"
prayed the Psalmist (cxxxix. 24). There is
one, and only one, road that leads Home.
Heaven is at the end of that way. There are
many attractive and alluring by-ways, but
only the one true way, and we need the
Comforter to guide us in that way. " When
He, the Spirit of truth, is come, He will
guide you," said Jesus, " guide you into all
truth " (John xvi. 13)—the truth about God,
about Jesus His Son, about salvation and
holiness, about sin and its certain and
unending consequences, about the shed
blood that saves from sin, about the way
of faith and the life of obedience and the
will of God and the joy set before us. It is
the way of the Cross, of duty, of lowly,
humble, faithful service; the way of love
and truth and justice and all right and holy
living; the way of patient well-being, for-
bearance and kindness, and the spirit that
forgives and gives and asks no reward but

the grace to give more fully, love more tenderly, believe more firmly, serve more wisely, hope more joyfully, and never to fail.

(4) *The Pentecostal Blessing is for power.* " Ye shall receive power, after that the Holy Ghost is come upon you," said Jesus (Acts i. 8). We are naturally weak in " the inner man." We fall before temptation. We faint with hopelessness, discouragement or fear in the presence of difficulty or danger. We flame with hasty temper or passion under provocation. We are puffed up with false views of our own ability or importance ; or we are cast down by a feeling of our own impotence. But when the Comforter comes He strengthens us in the inner man. He humbles us with a true view of our weakness, our ignorance, our foolishness and insufficiency, and then lifts us up with the revelation of God's sufficiency and eagerness to reinforce us at every point of our spiritual need.

I bow my knees unto the Father of our Lord Jesus Christ (wrote Paul), . . . that He would grant you, according to the riches of His glory, to be strengthened with might by His Spirit in the inner man (Eph. iii. 14, 16).

We should watch and pray and trustfully wait, daily and hourly and momentarily, for that inner strengthening by the Spirit, that we may be strong to work, to fight, to resist, to serve, to sacrifice, to suffer, to dare and bear up and press on joyfully and not grow weary nor fainthearted.

Before Pentecost Peter was ignorant of himself. So conceited was he that he rebuked Jesus for saying that He was to die on a cross; so cocksure of himself that he boasted that he would die with Jesus; and yet so inwardly weak that he denied Jesus when a maid pointed him out as one of the disciples, and he cursed and swore that he did not know Jesus. But when a few days later the Holy Ghost had come and strengthened him " in the inner man," he boldly preached Christ Jesus to the multitudes in Jerusalem. And when he and John were beaten and threatened and thrown into prison, they gloried that they were counted worthy to suffer and bear shame for Jesus. They were comforted, instructed, guided, and made inwardly strong to do and dare and bear and suffer—by the Pentecostal baptism.

*   *   *

" The baptism with the Holy Ghost is for power for service !" so many people think and say. And so it is. *But it is for far more !* The baptism *does* reinforce and empower the soul. The man or woman who is baptized with the Spirit is " endued with power from on high " (Luke xxiv. 49), and has *a spiritual energy and effectiveness which are not of this world*. Their lives and their words take on a strange, new influence and power which come from the active co-operation of an unseen Guest, a holy and Divine Presence abiding in love within them, and this fits them for the service of their Lord.

But service is not the *whole* purpose of man's being. What a man *is* is more important than what he *does*. Goodness is better than greatness. A man may do much and make a great name for himself, and end in Hell ; but a good man, who loves God and his fellow-men, though he may not be known beyond the street in which he lives, the factory in which he works, the place where he worships, he is on the way to Heaven, and is well known up there. There are those who are first who shall be last ; and there are last who shall be first.

The baptism of the Holy Ghost is to bring us into union with Christ, into loving fellowship with the Heavenly Father, to fit us snugly into God's great, complex scheme of life, and equip us for such service or sacrifice as falls to our lot. The busy house-wife, the burdened mother, the toiler in mine or factory, on farm or train or ship-board, the clerk at his desk, the merchant prince, the boot-black and the Prime Minister, the King and the President, the schoolboy and girl—each and all need the Pentecostal Blessing for daily life and duty, as much as does the Captain of a Salvation Army corps, the missionary in India or Africa, the General of The Salvation Army or the Archbishop of Canterbury, if they are to live worthy lives that shall glorify God and do their work in a spirit well pleasing to Him.

We each and all need the Blessing of Pentecost, not simply for service, but for holy, worthy living, for the perfecting and completing of character from which will flow influences which often are more effective than the busy activity which we call service.

A hard-headed business man saw a poor widow woman with her brood of fatherless children going to the house of God Sunday after Sunday, and one day it convicted him of his sin and neglect and turned him in repentance and faith to the Saviour. Her "patient continuance in well doing" (Rom. ii. 7), which was a fruit of the Spirit, was more effective than any word she could have spoken.

A lawyer came to his wife's pastor and asked to be received as a member of the church. The pastor was glad, for he had preached sermons to reach this man. So he asked, somewhat shamefacedly, which one of his sermons had brought him to decision.

" Well, pastor," replied the lawyer, " to tell the truth, it was not one of your sermons. A few Sundays ago I was leaving the church and found old coloured Auntie Blank haltingly trying to get down the icy steps, and I took her arm and helped her. Then she turned her black face, all radiant, up to mine, and asked, ' Do you love my Jesus ? ' It cut to my heart. I saw her peace and overflowing love and joy, in spite of her poverty and rheumatism, and it convicted me of my sin and led me to Christ."

The fruit of the Spirit, manifest in life and look and everyday, unpremeditated speech, often works more silently, deeply, effectively than our preaching ; and only the Pentecostal Blessing can produce this fruit unto perfection in our lives.

Many years ago I was campaigning in a little city in far-away Minnesota just at the time of the annual meeting of the Methodist Conference. The town was full of Methodist preachers, many of whom attended our Salvation Army open-air meetings, and some of whom came to our hall. Some of them invited me to come to their " love feast," or testimony meeting, at nine o'clock on Sunday morning, just before the bishop's great sermon, and give my testimony; which I did. After speaking for some time I was going to sit down, but they begged me to speak on, so I continued. Then the presiding elder, host of the Conference, came in, and seeing me in the pulpit he most peremptorily ordered me to sit down. The preachers protested, while my peace flowed like a river. I assured him I would be through in a moment, and I hurried out to my holiness meeting.

Several of the preachers said, " We have not believed in the Blessing, but that Salvationist has it, else instead of smiling and keeping calm and full of peace, he would have taken offence at that presiding elder." And leaving the bishop they came to our little hall, and in the holiness meeting came to the Mercy Seat for the Blessing. One of them received the fiery, cleansing, humbling baptism and became a witness to the Blessing and a flaming evangelist throughout all that region.

It was not my preaching alone, but the fruit of the Spirit that won him. *And it was not of me*. I am not by nature calm and peaceful. Quite the contrary. It was supernatural. My proud heart had been humbled to receive the Comforter, and graciously and in love He had come; and it was He in my heart who kept me peaceful

[56]

and calm, and to Him be the glory.
" Great peace have they which love Thy
law "—in whom the Comforter abides—
" and nothing shall offend them " (Ps. cxix.
165). Nothing. It is to cleanse and empower the soul and produce this heavenly
fruit in earth's harsh climate that the Pentecostal Blessing is given.

" The fruit of the Spirit is love, joy, peace,
longsuffering, gentleness, goodness, faith,
meekness, temperance " (Gal. v. 22). And
the Christian in whom this fruit—full, rich,
and ripe—is found has received his Pentecost, and, in spite of infirmities and human
frailties and limitations, is reproducing the
life of Jesus upon earth; and out of him,
most often unconsciously, flow influence
and power that are like " rivers of living
water " (John vii. 38) in desert lands. In
him Christ is magnified (Phil. i. 20) and the
Father is glorified (John xv. 8).

Have YOU *received the Holy Ghost since you
believed?* (Acts xix. 2).

III. THE GUEST OF THE SOUL

A FRIEND of mine said recently, "I like the term, 'Holy Ghost,' for the word Ghost in the old Saxon was the same as the word for Guest." Whether that be so or not, it may certainly be said that the Holy Ghost is the Holy Guest. He has come into the world and visits every heart, seeking admittance as a guest. He may come to the soul unbidden, but He will not come *in* unbidden. He may be unwelcome. He may be refused admission and turned away. But He comes. He is in the world like Noah's dove, looking for an abiding-place. He comes as a Guest, but as an abiding one, if received. He forces Himself upon no one. He waits for the open door and the invitation.

He comes gently. He comes in love. He comes on a mission of infinite good will, of mercy and peace and helpfulness and joy. He is the Advocate of the Father and of the Son to us men. He represents and executes the redemptive plans and purposes of the Triune God. As my old teacher, Daniel Steele, wrote, " He is the Executive of the Godhead."

The Holy Ghost convicts of sin. Men cease

to be self-complacent when He comes. Self-righteousness is seen to be a sheet too short to cover us ; our moral and spiritual nakedness is exposed. Our pride is rebuked and we are ashamed. Our self-conceit vanishes and we are abashed. Our eyes are opened, and we see how self-deceived we have been—how un-Christlike in our tempers, how corrupt in our desires, how selfish in our ambitions, how puffed up in our vainglory, how slow to believe, how quick to excuse ourselves and justify our own ways ; how far from God we have wandered, how unfit for Heaven we have become.

And He thus reveals us to ourselves in love that He may save us, as a wise and good physician shows us our disease in order to get our consent to be cured. But His supreme work of conviction is to convince us how hopelessly we miss the mark because we do not from the heart believe on and trust in Christ. This is the sin we do not recognize as sin until He convinces us of it : " Of sin, because they believe not on Me " (John xvi. 9).

The Holy Ghost convicts of righteousness. We no longer justify ourselves and condemn God. Our mouths are stopped. We see that God is true and righteous altogether, and in the presence of His holiness and righteousness, all our righteousness is seen to be as filthy rags. We can only cry, as did the leper, Unclean, I am unclean; oh, make me clean ! " If Thou wilt, Thou canst make me clean ! " (Luke v. 12). And then we see that Christ Jesus was " wounded for our transgressions, He was bruised for our iniquities : the chastisement of our peace was upon Him ; and with His stripes we are healed " (Isa. liii. 5) ; that He " bare our sins in His own body on the tree, that we, being dead to sins, should live unto righteousness " (1 Peter ii. 24) ; that He " suffered for sins, the just for the unjust " (1 Peter iii. 18) ; that God " hath made Him to be sin for us, who knew no sin ; that we might be made the righteousness of God in Him " (2 Cor. v. 21), that we might be able joyfully to sing :

> O Love, thou bottomless abyss,
>   My sins are swallowed up in thee
> Covered is my unrighteousness,
>   Nor spot of guilt remains on me,
> While Jesus' blood, through earth and skies,
> Mercy, free, boundless mercy, cries.

The Holy Ghost convicts of judgment ; of judgment present, now—bound up with and accompanying our every act, word, thought, intent and motive, as our shadow accompanies our body ; and of judgment to come—of judgment exact, final, irrevocable,

from which there is no escape and no appeal.
He convicts of judgment unto life : life full,
complete, eternal ; unto bliss : bliss overflowing, bliss ineffable, if we are found in
Christ, approved of God ; and of judgment
unto banishment : banishment unto outer
darkness, banishment eternal ; judgment
unto woe immeasurable, banishment into
shame unutterable, the harvest of our pride,
the reaping of our sin, if we are found out of
Christ, disapproved of God. The seed may
be small, but the harvest great. From little
seeds mighty trees and vast harvests do
grow.

When the Holy Ghost becomes the Holy
Guest *He opens the eyes of our understanding to
understand the Scriptures.* Without His aid
the Bible is just literature, and some of it is
dry and hopelessly uninteresting and not
understandable literature. But when He
removes the scales from our eyes and
illuminates its pages, it becomes most
precious, a new and living Book, in which
God speaks to men in love, in promise, in
precept, in types and symbols, in warning,
rebuke, entreaty and always in love, to save.
It reveals God. It comforts, rebukes,
inspires, convicts, converts, and rejoices
the heart. It is " sharper than any two-
edged sword," and proves itself to be " a
discerner of the thoughts and intents [inten-

tions and motives] of the heart " (Heb. iv. 12).

When the Holy Ghost becomes the Holy Guest in the yielded welcoming heart He dwells there ungrieved and with delight. " As the bridegroom rejoiceth over the bride " (Isa. lxii. 5), so He rejoices over that soul, while the soul has sweet, ennobling, purifying fellowship and communion with its Lord. He illuminates that soul; purifies, sanctifies, empowers it; instructs it, comforts it, protects it, adjusts it to all circumstances and crosses, and fits it for effective service, patient suffering, and willing sacrifice.

Some time ago my dear friend and comrade of many years, Commissioner Sowton, who has since gone to Heaven, was passing through New York with his devoted wife. He had only recently got well settled in his appointment in Australia, a country he enjoyed, where he felt at home, and whose people he had come to admire and love, when orders came to farewell and proceed to England to a new appointment.

To go from sunny Australia to foggy London in mid-winter was not pleasant; to leave a field and work and people he loved for the administration of men's social work, where all would be new and strange, was not what he expected or would have

chosen ; but he told me that the text, " Even
Christ pleased not Himself " (Rom. xv. 3),
kept whispering in his heart, and so with
perfect and glad resignation, and in great
peace, he and Mrs. Sowton were on their
way to their new home and tasks.

As he told me this, his face was as serene
as a summer's eve, and my own heart sensed
the Divine calm that possessed him, and was
refreshed and blessed. It was the indwelling
Holy Guest who whispered those words to
his heart and fitted him without murmuring
into this providence of God, and made him
so ready for service and so peaceful in
sacrifice.

When the Holy Guest abides within, the
soul does not shun the way of the Cross,
nor seek great things for itself. It is content
to serve in lowly as in lofty ways, in obscure
and hidden places as in open and con-
spicuous places where waits applause. To
wash a poor disciple's feet is as great a joy
as to command an army, to follow as to lead,
to serve as to rule—when the Holy Guest
abides within the soul. Then the soul does
not contend for or grasp and hold fast to
place and power. It glories rather in ful-
filling Paul's exhortation : " Let this mind
be in you, which was also in Christ Jesus,"
and it studies Paul's description and illustration of that mind :

Who, being in the form of God, thought it not robbery [or a thing to be grasped after and held fast] to be equal with God : but made Himself of no reputation [emptied Himself, put off His glory and equality with God], and took upon Him the form of a servant, and was made in the likeness of men : and being found in fashion as a man, He humbled Himself, and became obedient unto death, even the death of the cross " (Phil. ii. 6–8).

And having thus glimpsed the mind, the character of Christ, the soul yields itself eagerly to the Holy Guest to be conformed to that mind. That is its ambition, its whole desire, its joy and exceeding great reward. To do the will of the Master, to please Him, to win souls for Him, to serve and suffer and sacrifice for Him and with Him, is its great business; but to be like Him, to live in His favour, in fellowship and friendship with Him, is its life, its great and solemn joy.

When a guest comes into my home—a guest high-minded, wise, large of soul, pure of heart, generous in impulse—he imparts to me something of his own nobility. Mean things look meaner, low things sink lower, base things seem baser to his presence, and " whatsoever things are true, . . . honest, . . . just, . . . pure, . . . lovely, . . . of good report ; if there be any virtue, and if there be any praise " (Phil. iv. 8), these are the things upon which I would think and about which I would converse; these and these only are the worth-while things in his ennobling presence. But if this be so when a mere man, however upright and holy, comes in, how much more when God the Holy Ghost comes in!

Some people lay great stress upon the second coming of Christ as an incentive to fine and holy living, and I would not minimize this; but Jesus said: "At that day," when the Comforter has come in as the Holy Guest—" at that day ye shall know that I am in My Father, and ye in Me, and I in you" (John xiv. 20). In other words: when the Holy Guest abides within, the Father and the Son are there too; and what finer, more searching and sanctifying incentive to holy living can one have than this indwelling presence of Father, Son and Holy Ghost, as Guest of the Soul?

Finally, *the great work of this Holy Guest is to exalt Jesus*; to glorify Him who humbled Himself unto the shameful and agonizing death of the cross; to make us to see Him in all His beauty; to knit our hearts to Him in faith and love and loyalty, conform us to His image and fit us for His work.

The Holy Ghost as Guest within us does not concentrate our attention upon His own Person and work, but upon Jesus and His work and sacrifice for us. He does not glorify Himself. He whispers continually of Christ and His example. He points us to Jesus. He would have us "consider the Apostle and High Priest of our profession, Christ Jesus; who was faithful" (Heb. iii. 1, 2). He would have us "consider Him that endured such contradiction of sinners against Himself, lest"—when we are tired and harassed—lest we "be wearied and faint in" our "minds" (Heb. xii. 3), and feel our cross too heavy to bear. "Even Christ pleased not Himself," whispered He to my friend, who heard the sweet whisper and was content to follow and be as the Master.

When, after having been a Methodist pastor, I joined The Salvation Army, in the Training College I was set to black the boots of ignorant Cadets. I was tempted to feel it was a dangerous waste of my time, for which my Lord might hold me to account as He did the man who buried his talent, instead of putting it out at usury. Then the Holy Guest whispered to me of Jesus, and pointed me to Him washing the weary and soiled feet of His lowly disciples; and as I saw Jesus I was content. Any service for Him and His lowly ones, instead of abasing, exalted me.

What we need evermore, in every place, at all times, in prosperity and adversity, in health and in sickness, in joy and sorrow, in sunshine and shadow, in wealth or grinding poverty, in comfort and distress, in the fellowship and love of friends and in desolation and loneliness, in victory and defeat, in liberty or in prison, in deliverance or temptation, in life and in death ; what we need and shall ever need, is to see Jesus, and, seeing Him, to walk in His footsteps,

who did no sin, neither was guile found in His mouth : who, . . . when He suffered, He threatened not ; but committed Himself to Him that judgeth righteously (1 Peter ii. 22, 23).

And this the Holy Guest delighteth to help us to do as we " watch and pray," as we " trust and obey." To those, and those only, who obey Jesus is this Holy Guest given (Acts v. 32), and when He is given it is that He may abide as Comforter, Counsellor, Helper, Friend.

IV.—THE TRIAL OF FAITH
WROUGHT INTO EXPERIENCE

THE world owes an immeasurable debt to Christianity for its treasures of music and song. Jesus sang (Matt. xxvi. 30). Oh, to have heard Him! And in his Letters, especially, to the Ephesians and Colossians, Paul exhorts the Christians to speak to themselves, "teaching and admonishing one another in psalms and hymns and spiritual songs, singing with grace in your hearts to the Lord," and "making melody in your hearts to the Lord" (Col. iii. 16; Eph. v. 19). They were to sing to be heard not of men only, but of the Lord Himself.

Every great revival of religion results in a revival of singing and of the composition of both music and song. The Franciscan revival in the thirteenth century was marked by exultant singing. And so it was in the days of Luther, of the Wesleys, of William Booth, and of Moody. And so it will always be.

The joys, the faith, the hopes and aspirations, the deepest desires, the love and utter devotion, and the sweet trust of the Christian find noblest and freest expression in music and song. And yet it is probable that in no way do people more frequently and yet unconsciously stultify, befool and deceive themselves, and actually lie to each other and to God, than in the public singing of songs and hymns.

Languidly, lustily, thoughtlessly in song they profess a faith they do not possess, a love and devotion their whole life falsifies, a joy their lack of radiance on the face and of light in the eye contradicts. They sing, "Oh, how I love Jesus!" while their hearts are far from Him, with no intention of doing the things that please Him; or:

> I've wondrous peace through trusting,
>   A well of joy within;
> This rest is everlasting,
>   My days fresh triumphs bring—

while they are restless and defeated; or:

> Take my life, and let it be
> Consecrated, Lord, to Thee;
> Take my moments and my days,
> Let them flow in ceaseless praise—

while they live selfishly and spend much of their time in murmurings and complainings, instead of in praise.

It is a solemn thing to stand before God and sing such songs.

[69]

We should think. A hush should be upon our spirits, for we are standing upon holy ground, where mysteries are all about us, enshrouding us, while the Angel of the Lord looks upon us through pillar of cloud and fire, and devils leer and lurk to entrap and overthrow us.

Nearly fifty years ago, at The Salvation Army's Training Home, at Clapton, we Cadets were singing:

> My will be swallowed up in Thee;
> Light in Thy light still may I see
> In Thine unclouded face.
> Called the full strength of trust to prove . . .

and there my heart cried out, " Yes, Lord, let me prove the full strength of trust ! "

And then I was hushed into deep questioning and prayer, for a whisper within me, deep within, asked: " Can you, will you, endure the tests, the trials, that alone can prove the full strength of trust ? A feather's weight may test the strength of an infant or an invalid, but heavier and yet heavier weights alone can test the full strength of a man. Will you bear patiently, without murmuring or complaining or fainting, the trials I permit to come upon you, which alone can prove the full strength of your trust and train it for larger service and yet greater trials ? "

My humbled heart dared not say, " I can,"

but only, " By Thy grace I will." And then
we continued to sing :

> My will be swallowed up in Thee
> . . . .
> Let all my quickened heart be love;
> My spotless life be praise.

And my whole soul consented to any
trial which the Lord in His wisdom and love
might permit to come upon me. I willed
to be wholly the Lord's ; to endure, to
" bear up and steer right onward " in the
face of every tempest that might blow, every
whelming sea that might threaten to engulf
me, every huge Goliath who might mock
and vow he would destroy me. I was not
jubilant : my soul was awed into silence,
but also into strong confidence and a deep
rest of quiet faith.

I felt sure from that hour that if I was to
do a man's work, to be a saint or soldier of
Christ, a winner of souls, and a conqueror
on life's battlefields, then I was not to be a
pampered pet of the Lord : that I must not
expect favours ; that my path was not to be
strewn with roses ; that acclaiming multitudes were not to cheer and crown me ; that
I must walk by faith, not sight ; that I must
be faithful and hold fast that which God had
given me ; that I must still pray when
Heaven seemed shut and God not listening ;
that I must rejoice in tribulation and glorify

my Lord in the fire; that I must keep hot
when others grew cold; that I must stand
alone when others ran away; that I must
look to no man for my example, but that
I myself should seek always to be an example
to all men; that I must stand on instant
guard against the lure of the world, the
insurgence and insistence of the flesh and the
wiles of the Devil; that I must not become
sarcastic, cynical, suspicious, or supercilious,
but have the love that thinketh no evil,
beareth all things, believeth all things,
hopeth all things, endureth all things, and
never faileth; that I must not be seduced
by flattery, nor frightened by frowns. I felt
that, while esteeming others better than
myself (Phil. ii. 3), and in honour preferring
others before myself (Rom. xii. 10), and
while I was not to be wise in my own
conceits (Rom. xii. 16), yet I was in no sense
to permit my own personality to be sub-
merged in the mass; that I must be myself,
stand on my own feet, fulfil my own task, bear
my own responsibility, answer at last for my
own soul, and stand or fall, when the Judgment books are opened, by my own record.

That moment when we sang those words
was to me most solemn and sacred, and not
to be forgotten. There God set His seal
upon my consenting soul, for service, for
suffering, for sacrifice. From that moment

life became a thrilling adventure in fellowship with God, in friendship and companionship with Jesus. Everything that has come into my life from that moment has, in some way, by God's sanctifying touch and unfailing grace, enriched me. It may have impoverished me on one side, but it has added to my spiritual wealth on the other, as Jacob's withered thigh, Joseph's slavery and imprisonment, Moses' enforced banishment from Pharaoh's court, and Paul's thorn and shipwrecks and stonings and imprisonments, enriched them.

Pain has come to me, but in it I have always found some secret pleasure and compensation. Sorrow and bereavement have thrown me back upon God and deepened and purified my joy in Him. Agony, physical and mental, have led to some unexpected triumph of grace and faith, some enlargement of sympathy and of power to understand and bless others. Loss and gain, loneliness and love, light and darkness, trials and things hard or impossible to understand—everything has brought its own blessing as my soul has bowed to and accepted the yoke of Jesus and refused to murmur or complain, but has received the daily providences of life as God's training school for faith, for patience, for steadfastness and love.

Paul was right—and my soul utters a deep Amen—when he wrote : " All things work together for good to them that love God, to them who are called according to His purpose " (Rom. viii. 28). Listen to Paul's record of some of the " all things " which worked together for his good. He had been ridiculed and treated with scorn by his enemies as an Apostle and minister, and he replies :

Are they ministers of Christ ? (I speak as a fool) I am more ; in labours more abundant, in stripes above measure, in prisons more frequent, in deaths oft.

Of the Jews five times received I forty stripes save one. Thrice was I beaten with rods, once was I stoned, thrice I suffered shipwreck, a night and a day I have been in the deep ; in journey-ings often [long and dangerous, over bandit-infested roads], in perils of waters [on stormy seas and icy mountain torrents and unbridged rivers], in perils of robbers [in Balkan hills and Cilician mountain passes], in perils by mine own countrymen [the Jews were always lying in wait for him in every city], in perils by the heathen, in perils in the city, in perils in the wilderness, in perils in the sea, in perils among false brethren ; in weariness and painfulness [long journeys wearied him, and stonings, beatings, whippings and holding on grimly to a spar after ship-wreck, while the surges of the sea beat upon him to and fro for a night and a day, must have meant excruciating pain], in watchings often, in hunger and thirst, in cold and nakedness.

Beside those things that are without, that which cometh upon me daily, the care of all the churches (2 Cor. xi. 23–28).

What a list of " all things," and yet it is not complete ! A study of his Corinthian Letters reveals much more of his mental and spiritual trials and conflicts which meant unmeasured suffering to his sensitive soul, so chaste in its purity, so keenly alive to all the finest and loftiest views of life, and so hungry for human as well as Divine love and fellowship. This is the man who glories in his tribulations, because they work in him patience, experience, hope (Rom. v. 3, 4), and declares that in all things he is more than conqueror (Rom. viii. 37). Indeed, he calls these things a " light affliction, which is but for a moment " (2 Cor. iv. 17).

He looks at them in the light of Eternity and they are so swallowed up in that vastness, that infinitude, that he says they are " but for a moment." And then he adds that this affliction " worketh for us "—our slave, working out

for us a far more exceeding and eternal weight of glory ; while we look not at the things which are seen, but at the things which are not seen : for the things which are seen are temporal

[fleeting, soon to pass away and be forgotten] ;
but the things which are not seen are eternal
(2 Cor. iv. 17, 18).

Paul says, " *We know* "—his uncertainties,
doubts, fears, questionings, had all vanished,
being swallowed up in knowledge—" we
know that all things work together for good
to them that love God."

But how did he know ? How had Paul
reached such happy assurance ? He knew
by faith. He believed God, and light on
dark problems streamed into his soul
through faith.

He knew by *joyful union with the risen
Christ,* who had conquered death and the
grave. This union was so real that Christ's
victory was his victory also.

He knew in part *by experience.* Paul had
suffered much, and by experience he had
found all things in the past working for his
good, enriching his spiritual life through
the abounding grace of his Lord ; and this
gave him assurance for " all things " and for
all the future. Nothing could really harm
him while he was in the Divine will, in the
eternal order ; while he was a branch in the
living Vine, a member of Christ's body
(Rom. xii. 5 ; 1 Cor. xii. 20–27).

Listen to him :

Who shall separate us from the love of
Christ ? shall tribulation, or distress, or persecu-

tion, or famine, or nakedness, or peril, or sword?
. . . Nay, in all these things we are more than
conquerors through Him that loved us (Rom.
viii. 35, 37).

Hear him again :

We glory in tribulations also : knowing that
tribulation worketh patience [steadfastness] ;
and patience, experience ; and experience, hope :
and hope maketh not ashamed ; because the
love of God is shed abroad in our hearts by the
Holy Ghost which is given unto us (Rom. v. 3-5).

Hear him yet once more :

I am persuaded, that neither death, nor life,
nor angels, nor principalities, nor powers, nor
things present, nor things to come, nor height,
nor depth, nor any other creature, shall be able
to separate us from the love of God, which is in
Christ Jesus our Lord (Rom. viii. 38, 39).

Any and everything, present and future,
which wrought in him patience, experience
of God's love, and hope, he was sure was
working for his good, and he welcomed it
with rejoicing, for it came bearing gifts of
spiritual riches. That is how he knew. We
may believe what is revealed in the Bible
about this, and enter into peace, great
peace ; but we come to know, as did Paul,
by putting God and life to the test—by
experience.

I happened to be present when a young
wife and mother was weeping bitter tears of

anguish. An older wife and mother, with a face like the morning, full of Heaven's own peace, who had herself wept bitter tears of anguish, put her arms around the younger woman and in tender and wise words of perfect assurance comforted her. And as I noted the gentleness, the wisdom, the calmness, the moral strength of the elder woman, I thought to myself, " Ah, her trials that were so painful, her tears that were so bitter, worked for her good ; left her enlarged in heart, enriched in experience and knowledge, sweetened in character, wise in sympathy, calm in storm, perfect in peace, with a spirit at home and at rest in God while yet in the body."

And I looked forward with joy in the hope that the younger woman, believing on Jesus, patiently submitting to chastenings and trials as opportunities for the exercise and the discipline of faith, would enter into an experience of God's love and faithfulness that would leave her spirit for ever strengthened, sweetened, enriched, and fitted to comfort and strengthen others. And so, after years, it proved to be.

Our true good in this and all worlds is spiritual ; and trials, afflictions, losses, sorrows, chastenings, borne with patience and courage and in faith, will surely develop in us spiritual graces and " the peaceable fruit of righteousness" (Heb. xii. 11), which are never found in those who know no trial or sorrow, whose sky is never overcast, whose voyage over life's sea is never troubled by storm and hurricane, whose soldiering is only on dress parade and never in deadly battle, or who, facing storm or battle, flee away and so escape it.

Holiness of heart does not insure us against those untoward and painful things which try our faith, but it does prepare us for the trial; while the patient endurance of trial reveals to ourselves, to angels, to devils, to men, the reality of our faith and the purity and integrity of our hearts and the grace and faithfulness of our Lord.

When Abraham was tried in the offering up of Isaac, "the angel of the Lord" said, "Now I know that thou fearest God, seeing thou hast not withheld thy son, thine only son from me" (Gen. xxii. 12). And again and again the most obstinate opponents of Christianity have been conquered by the patient endurance and the radiant joy of suffering Christians. It was not only so in the days of far-off persecutions—in Rome, when Christians were thrown to the wild beasts, roasted over slow fires, tortured in every conceivable way; but in our own day, and in the history of the Salvation Army, the blood of the martyrs, the patience and triumphant joy of our soldiers, have won the hardest sinners to Jesus.

Paul looked upon his sufferings as a part of the sufferings of Christ, as though Christ's sufferings did not end upon the cross, but were completed in the sufferings of His disciples. Paul writes : I now " rejoice in my sufferings for you, and fill up that which is behind of the afflictions of Christ in my flesh for His body's sake, which is the church " (Col. i. 24).

Happy are we if we can receive all suffering in that spirit, whether it be suffering of body, mind or soul. It will then work for our good and through us for the good of others, whether or not we can understand how it is to do so.

It will purge us of vanity ; it will deepen us in humility, enlarge us in sympathy, and make us more fruitful in the graces of the Spirit.

How bitter that cup no tongue can conceive,
Which He drank quite up that sinners might live.
His way was much rougher and darker than mine :
Did Christ, my Lord, suffer, and shall I repine ?

Since all that I meet shall work for my good,
The bitter is sweet, the medicine is food ;
Though painful at present, 'twill cease before long,
And then, oh, how pleasant the conqueror's song !

V. A PERFECT-HEARTED PEOPLE

GOD is looking for people whose hearts are perfect towards Him — a perfected-hearted people; so there is a kind of perfection required of His people by God.

A friend of mine asked me some time ago whether I believed in and taught perfection. I replied that that depended upon what he meant by the term " perfection."

If he meant *absolute* perfection, I did not; nor did I believe in the possession by men of *angelic* perfection; nor yet in their realizing *such perfection as Adam* must have originally *possessed*.

God alone is *absolutely perfect* in all His attributes, and to such perfection we can never hope to attain. Then there is a perfection possessed by the angels, which we shall never have in this world. Adam also had certain perfections of body and mind which are out of our reach.

There is, however, a perfection which we are given to understand God requires in us. It is a perfection not of head but of heart; not of knowledge, but of goodness, of humility, of love, of faith. Such a perfection

God desires us to have, and such a perfection
we may have.

In saying this I cannot be accused of
being a crank or a fanatic, for I am proclaim-
ing only the plain, simple truth as it is
revealed in God's word, and we ought to
desire to rise up to all the privileges God
has conferred upon us.

"Be ye therefore perfect, even as your
Father which is in Heaven is perfect," said
Jesus (Matt. v. 48). What sort of perfection
is this which we are to possess? God is a
Spirit; we are simply men and women.
And further, "No man hath seen God at
any time" (John i. 18). How then are we
to know what that perfection is which He
requires of us—a perfection which it is
possible for men and women to manifest?
In this, Jesus is our pattern. It is true that
"no man hath seen God at any time," but
"the only begotten Son . . . He hath
declared Him" (John i. 18)—that is, manifested the Father's nature and perfections in
a human life which we can see and understand.

This perfection of heart, of purity, of
goodness, was seen in Jesus in several
particulars, and in these we are to follow
His example.

First : We are to be *perfectly submitted to
God.* We are to come to the place where

we no longer fight against God's will; where we do not complain, nor talk back, nor resist, but yield in perfect submission to all His will.

In the terrible *General Slocum* disaster in New York Harbour some years ago, almost all the mothers and children of one church lost their lives. The next Sunday the bereaved fathers and husbands came to the church, and the pastor, who had lost his whole family, rose and said, " The Lord gave, and the Lord hath taken away; blessed be the name of the Lord " (Job i. 21). These men were perfectly submissive to God in their hearts, and they did not fail God in the hour of their suffering and trial, and fight against His providences.

It is possible to be submitted to God in this way. We may not understand God's providences, but we can say " Amen " to them from our hearts.

Second : Like Jesus, we may *perfectly trust God.* We may possess a confidence in God that holds out in ways which we do not understand, like the confidence that a very little child has in its parents ; that will trust with all the heart.

Job was rich, prosperous and happy. Then trouble came. He was afflicted, he lost his children, he lost his property, and his herds were carried off by marauders.

And what did Job do? He did not complain and blame God, but said, " The Lord gave, and the Lord hath taken away; blessed be the name of the Lord." And when his backslidden wife advised him to curse God and die, Job defended God's way and said, " Thou speakest as one of the foolish women speaketh. What? Shall we receive good at the hand of God, and shall we not receive evil?" And "in all this did not Job sin with his lips " (Job ii. 10).

Then his friends tried to shake his confidence, and Job—afflicted, full of pain, poor, and bereaved of his children—seemed to be forsaken by God; but he looked up from his ash heap and exclaimed, " Though He slay me, yet will I trust in Him " (Job xiii. 15).

It is always so with the perfect-hearted man. I want my friends to trust me, and if they failed to do so when I was out of their sight it would break my heart. So God wants us to trust Him where we cannot see Him.

Paul and Silas, on one of their missionary journeys, were arrested and placed in one of those loathsome Roman prisons—in the inmost, wet, slimy, foul dungeon—with the wounds on their backs from the scourging they had just received gaping wide, and with their feet in the stocks. But they did not worry and complain and determine to go home when they were released. They sang and praised the Lord.

That is the kind of spirit God wants His people to possess ; a spirit that will rejoice with a perfect trust in Him under adversity.

Third : God desires His people to be *perfect in love* ; to love Him perfectly. We are not expected to love God with the heart of an archangel, for we are only poor humble men with limited power to love, but God does expect us to love with all *our* hearts—with all our power to love.

The little child is to love with all its power ; and as the powers develop and grow, our love is to develop and grow apace with our power to love ; but we are always to love with all the heart.

Fourth : There must be *perfect loyalty.* Love is not an emotion—a happy feeling ; it is not something on the surface ; it is a deep principle, revealing itself in perfect loyalty to God.

What constitutes a perfect son or a perfect wife ? Here is a big, ignorant young man. He could not shine in a drawing-room. He is hard-working, rough, un-cultured, and awkward, and in the eyes of the world is a most imperfect man. But he has a dear old mother whom he loves. He works to give her his meagre wages at the

[85]

end of the week; he carries up the coal; and when his day's work is done he comes home to cheer his old mother with his presence. He does all he can to make her latter days comfortable and happy.

Now he is a very imperfect man, but his mother would tell you with pride, " He is my perfect son." What makes him a perfect son? Perfect loyalty to his old mother.

So a man has a perfect heart when it beats in perfect loyalty to God—wholly yielded up to fulfil all His purposes. He may be very imperfect as a man, and his imperfections may be apparent to every one; he may blunder and make many mistakes; he may be ignorant and uncultured—yet God looks down and counts him a perfect-hearted man. When God sees a heart perfect in loyalty to Him, He overlooks many mistakes and blunders of the head.

Fifth: God also requires of us *perfect obedience*. Our performance may not always be perfect, but our spirit may be perfect.

My little boy, with his heart beating high to help his papa and do what I want him to do, goes into the garden to pull the weeds from among the vegetables; but he comes to the corn, and he doesn't know the difference between corn and weeds, and while pulling up the weeds he also pulls up my corn.

When I come home he runs to me, with eyes dancing, bursting to tell me how he has helped me by weeding the garden. I go out and find that, while he has weeded the garden, he has also pulled up my sweet corn. But I see that he has done it with a heart full of desire to please his father, and that the trouble has not been with his heart, but with his ignorant little head; and, seeing his perfect little heart, I press him to my breast and call him my little man. This is the kind of perfection God wants in us—perfect obedience of the heart.

God's eyes are in all parts of the earth, seeking for men with hearts perfect toward Him, in submission, in trust, in love, in obedience; and when He finds such a man He reveals Himself to Him and shows Himself on behalf of that man.

Now let me ask you, what kind of heart have you? Have you submitted to Him? Have you consecrated yourself wholly to Him? Have you put all your powers at His disposal? Have you let Him have all His way with you? How anger and pride and selfishness and uncleanness must grieve Him! The perfect-hearted man has put all these things away.

How can I put away these things that seem to be a part of my very being? How can I change the colour of my eyes or add a cubit to my stature ? I cannot ! Work as I will, I shall always fail to change my moral nature. But God can. It is His work.

If we go down before Him in complete humility and say, " Lord, I am willing to have my heart changed. Though it may mean that I shall be despised and hated and persecuted, I will take up my cross ; I will crucify myself. I am willing that my selfishness and pride and hate and uncleanness shall be taken from me, and that Thou shalt reign in me and create in me a clean heart, perfect in its love, submission, loyalty, trust, and obedience"—if we will say that to Him, He will answer our prayer to-day, now, this moment, if we will but believe.

VI. A THIRTEENTH-CENTURY
SALVATIONIST

MOST of the Ten Commandments can be made into laws of the land by legislative enactment, but not so the Sermon on the Mount. It is not only a sin, it is a crime, a breach of law, to murder and steal. But no statesman has ever yet passed a law compelling men to be poor in spirit, meek, merciful, pure of heart, loving to enemies, and glad when lied about and persecuted. A man may be restrained by the strong hand of the law from stealing or committing murder; but he can be constrained only by grace to be meek and lowly in heart, to bless them that curse him, to pray for them that despitefully use him, and to love them that hate him.

" The law was given by Moses, but grace and truth came by Jesus Christ " (John i. 17). He was " full of grace and truth " (John i. 14). When His heart broke on Calvary it was like the breaking of Mary's alabaster box of ointment. And when He poured out the Holy Spirit at Pentecost, rivers of grace and truth began to stream forth to every land, to all people.

The nature-religions and philosophies of

the Gentile world, and the religion of the
Scribes and Pharisees, sunk into legal forms
and ceremonies, were powerless to give
peace to troubled consciences, strength to
slaves of vice and corruption, or life to
souls dead in trespasses and sin. But this is
just what the grace of God in Christ did.
It met and fitted the moral and spiritual
needs of men as light meets the eye, as the
skin fits the hand.

When Paul went to luxurious, licentious
Corinth and preached Christ to the revelling
populace, lo! fornicators, idolaters, adul-
terers, sodomites, thieves, covetous people,
drunkards and revellers became saints. Their
eyes were opened, their darkness vanished,
their chains fell off, and they received
" beauty for ashes, the oil of joy for mourning, the garment of praise for the spirit of
heaviness " (Isa. lxi. 3). Christ made them
free. They loved each other. They lived
in close association with each other, but they
did not shut themselves away from their
unsaved neighbours. They went everywhere declaring the good news of redeeming
love and uttermost salvation in Christ.

But not all who named the name of Christ
departed from iniquity. Heresies crept in.
Persecutions arose. The awful corruptions
and subtle philosophies of the heathen world
undermined the morals, weakened the cour-

age, and dimmed or destroyed the faith of many. The whole social and political order of the ancient world began to crumble. The Roman empire fell before the assaults of northern barbarians, and the Dark Ages supervened. The secret of salvation and sanctification by faith, which made Paul's converts in Corinth victorious over the proud and putrid world in which they lived, the flesh which had enslaved them and the Devil who had deceived them, was largely if not wholly lost.

Earnest souls, sick of sin, weary of strife, and ignorant of the way of victorious faith in an indwelling Christ, fled to the desert and wilderness to escape temptation. Many of them became hermits, living solitary lives on pillars in the desert and in dens and caves of the earth, while others formed monastic communities of monks and nuns. They harked back to the grim austerity and asceticism of Elijah and John the Baptist, and lost the sweet reasonableness and holy naturalness of Jesus. In the solitude of desert dens and the darkness of wilderness caves and on the tops of lonely pillars they kept painful vigil and fought bitter battles with devils. With prolonged fastings and flagellations they struggled to overcome the unsanctified passions of the flesh.

There were saints among these seekers,

who found God and kept sacred learning and faith alive. It was the hermit St. Jerome who translated the Scriptures into the common language, giving us the version known as the Vulgate. It was the monk Thomas à Kempis who wrote " The Imitation of Christ." While some of the sweetest and most stirring hymns of Christendom leaped forth from glad and loving hearts, in monasteries of the Dark Ages. Those ages were dark, but not wholly dark.

As the iron empire of Rome, corroded and rusted by luxury and utterly corrupt vices, began to crumble and fall before the fierce, barbaric hordes of the north, feudalism sprang up and the great mass of men became serfs who tilled the fields and fought the wars of petty lords who lived in castles overlooking the towns and villages that dotted the plains. Towns and cities torn and reddened by internal factional strife made war on each other. The baron made war on his enemy, the rich abbot, and endowed and adorned his castle and church with spoils of his petty warfare. The clergy were generally greedy and corrupt. Poverty, illiteracy, filth and disease were universal. Brigands infested the forests and mountains, and pitiful, loathsome lepers begged for alms along the highways.

It was at the end of a thousand years of

such dimness and darkness, when was breaking a new dawn which he was greatly to hasten, that St. Francis of Assisi appeared. He was the son of a prosperous Italian cloth merchant and of a gentle and devout French lady who probably sprang from the nobility. A beautiful, courteous lad, with flashing eyes and equally flashing spirit, who sang the songs of the troubadours in his mother's native tongue, delighted in the sports and revelry and dare-devil doings of the youth of the town—such was Francis Bernadone. Little did he seem to have in him the stuff of a saint who should transform the Christendom of his day and hold the wondering and affectionate gaze of seven centuries. His father was a tradesman, but he was rich and free-handed with his dashing and attractive son.

The boy was lavish with money, courteous and gay of spirit, which made him the friend and companion of the young nobility who dwelt in castles. War broke out between Assisi and the city of Perugia, so Francis, burning with the pride of youth and the fires of patriotism, went forth with the young noblemen and their bands of serfs to fight the enemy. But the battle went against the Assisians, and a company of the leaders, with Francis, were captured and spent a year in prison.

The youthful aristocrats, deprived of liberty, languished, but Francis, whom they kept among them, never lost his spirit, but cheered them with his kindness, his gaiety, and his songs. He laughed and sang and made merry, and possibly half in jest but more in earnest, through some strange youthful premonition, he assured them that he would one day be a great prince, with his name on the lips of all men. Little did he or they suspect what kind of a prince he would be, or the nature of the acclaim with which men would greet him.

Months of sickness followed his imprisonment. He began to think on the things that are eternal, the things of the spirit. Recovered from his illness, he went forth again on a fine steed, in glittering armour, to war. But, for some rather obscure reason, he returned and fell into strange meditative moods. His companions suspected that it was an affair of the heart, and asked him if he was dreaming of a lady-love. He admitted that he was—a fairer love than they had ever imagined: *Lady Poverty!* He was thinking of giving up all for Christ.

One day, while Francis was serving a customer in his father's shop, a beggar came in and asked for alms in the name of God. Francis, busy with his customer, sent him away empty-handed, but afterwards said to himself, "If he had asked in the name of some nobleman, how promptly and generously I should have responded. But he asked in the name of the Lord, and I sent him away with nothing!" Leaving the shop, he ran after the beggar and lavished money upon him, and from that day he was the unfailing friend of beggars and all the poor.

Lepers were peculiarly repulsive to him, and he stood in a kind of fear of them. One day when riding he met a leper, and a fear he would not have felt on a field of battle gripped him. He rode past the poor creature and then, ashamed of himself, he won a greater victory than ever was won by armed warriors on a field of blood. He wheeled his horse about and returned, and leaping down he kissed the leper and gave him all the money he had with him. Joy filled his heart, and ever after he was the friend, the benefactor and the frequent nurse and companion of lepers.

He was a creature of generous, self-sacrificing impulse, but once he yielded to the impulse it became a life-long principle, and he served it with unfailing devotion of a lover to his mistress. As yet, however, like little Samuel, he "did not . . . know the Lord, neither was the word of the Lord yet revealed unto him" (1 Sam. iii. 7). But one day he was praying before the altar in a poor, half-ruined little church : " Great and glorious God, and Thou, Lord Jesus, I pray, shed abroad Thy light in the darkness of my mind. Be found of me, O Lord, so that in all things I may act only in accordance with Thy Holy Will." His eyes were upon a crucifix as he prayed, and it seemed to him that the eyes of the Saviour met his. The place suddenly became a holy place, and he was in the presence of the Lord and Saviour as was Moses when he drew near the burning bush on Horeb.

The sacred Victim seemed alive, and as a Voice spoke to Moses from the bush, so a wondrous, sweet, ineffable Voice seemed to speak from the crucifix to the longing soul of Francis, bidding him repair the church that was falling into decay and ruin. From that day he was assured that Christ knew him, heard him, loved him, and wanted his service. He could say : "I am my Beloved's, and my Beloved is mine."

Francis was essentially a man of action rather than of contemplation, so instead of retiring to a hermit's lodge in the desert or a monastery on some hill-top, he sallied forth at once to repair the little church of St. Damien in which he had been praying and had heard the Voice. He begged stones and carried them himself, repairing the church with his own hands, and when that was completed he repaired yet another church. It had not yet dawned upon him that the Voice was calling him to repair, not the four walls of a church made with hands, but the spiritual Church with its living stones not built with hands.

His proud and disappointed father fell upon him, beat him, and imprisoned him in his home; but during the absence of his father his mother released him, and he returned to the church, where he lived with the priest, wearing, instead of his gay clothing, a hair shirt and a rough brown robe tied around him with a rope, which was later to become the uniform of the myriad brothers of the Franciscan Order. He worked or begged for his bread and in Assisi was looked upon as a madman. His father and brother cursed him when they saw him.

He publicly renounced all right to his patrimony and adopted utter poverty as one of the rules of his life. He made poverty one of the rules—indeed, the most distinctive rule—of the Order which he founded. And later, when the Bishop of Assisi gently reproved him and argued that he should not go to such an extreme, he silenced the Bishop, who had trouble with his own riches, by shrewdly replying, "If we own property we must have laws and arms to defend them, and this will destroy love out of our hearts."

In a short time—as with a true Salvationist, with any true Christian—the sincerity, the sweetness, the joy and devotion of his life began to disarm criticism, win approval, and cause searchings of heart in many of his fellow townsmen.

His first convert was a wealthy man who had been impressed by his joyous, simple life. He invited Francis to spend the night with him, and only simulated sleep that he might watch the young man. When Francis thought he was asleep, he knelt by his bedside and spent most of the night in prayer. Next morning Bernardo, who became one of the most noted and devout of the brothers, decided to sell all, give to the poor, and cast in his lot with Francis.

A third, named Pietro, joined himself to them, and the three went to church where, after praying and examining the Scriptures, they adopted as the rule of their new life the words of Jesus:

If thou wilt be perfect, go and sell that thou hast, and give to the poor, and thou shalt have treasure in heaven: and·come and follow Me (Matt. xix. 21).

Jesus, having called the twelve,

[98]

gave them power and authority over all devils, and to cure diseases. And He sent them to preach the Kingdom of God. . . . And He said unto them, Take nothing for your journey, neither staves, nor scrip, neither bread, neither money ; neither have two coats apiece.

And whatsoever house ye enter into, there abide, and thence depart.

And whosoever will not receive you, when ye go out of that city, shake off the very dust from your feet for a testimony against them.

And they departed, and went through the towns, preaching the gospel, and healing every where (Luke ix. 1–6).

The literal strictness with which Francis and his early disciples followed and enforced the rule of utter poverty gave them great freedom from care, great freedom of movement, and much joy. But, later, this led to much strife and division in the Order, the beginnings of which in his lifetime saddened the last days of the saint.

The Pope sanctioned his Rule and granted him and the members of the Order the right to preach. Like the early disciples they went everywhere testifying, singing, preaching, labouring with their hands for food, and, when unable to get work, not hesitating to ask from door to door for bread.

At first they were scorned and often beaten, but they gloried in tribulation. " My brothers, commit yourselves to God with all your cares and He will care for you," said Francis, and they went with joy, strictly observing his instructions :

Let us consider that God in His goodness has called us not merely for our own salvation, but also for that of many men, that we may go through all the world exhorting men, more by our example than by our words, to repent*of their sins and keep the commandments. Be not fearful because we appear little and ignorant. Have faith in God, that His Spirit will speak in and by you.

You will find men, full of faith, gentleness, and goodness, who will receive you and your words with joy ; but you will find others, and in great numbers, faithless, proud, blasphemers, who will speak evil of you, resisting you and your words. Be resolute, then, to endure everything with patience and humility.

Have no fear, for very soon many noble and learned men will come to you ; they will be with you preaching to kings and princes and to a multitude of people. Many will be converted to the Lord all over the world, who will multiply and increase His family.

How like William Booth that sounds !

And what he preached, Francis practised to the end. He died prematurely, surrounded by his first followers, exhausted, blind and, at his own request, stripped, but for a hair shirt, and laid upon the bare ground. His Rule, his Order, his life and example were a stern and mighty rebuke to the wealth, the greed and the laziness of the priests and the monks. But he exhorted his brethren not to judge others, not to condemn or be severe, but to honour them, give them all due respect and pray for them, remembering that some whom they might think to be members of the Devil would yet become members of Christ.

Within a brief time five thousand friars in brown robes were going everywhere with their glad songs, their burning exhortations, their simple testimony and sacrificial lives, and all who met them met with a spiritual adventure not to be forgotten. In Spain some of them fell upon martyrdom. They went to Germany, France, and to far Scandinavia, where they built the great cathedral of Upsala. Francis himself went to the Holy Land with the crusaders, and at the risk of his life, with two of his brothers boldly entered the camp of the Saracens and sought to convert the Saracen leader and his host. In this he failed, but he made a deep impression on the followers of Mohammed.

Once he was called to preach before the Pope and the College of Cardinals. He carefully prepared his sermon, but when he attempted to deliver it he became confused, frankly confessed his confusion, forgot his prepared address, threw himself upon the Lord, and spoke from his heart as moved by the Spirit—spoke with such love and fire that he burned into all hearts and melted his august audience to many tears. Long before Hus and Luther appeared, thundering against the abuses of the Church, he wrought a great reformation by love, by simplicity, and self-sacrifice. He was a kindred spirit of George Fox and John Wesley and William Booth, and would have gloried in their fellowship.

After seven centuries his words are still as sweet as honey, as searching as fire, as penetrating and revealing as light. One winter's day, bitterly cold, he was journeying with a Brother Leo, when he said: "May it please God that the Brothers Minor (the 'Little Brothers,' the name he adopted for the Franciscan Order) all over the world may give a great example of holiness and edification. But not in this is the perfect joy. If the Little Brothers gave sight to the blind, healed the sick, cast out demons, gave hearing to the deaf, or even raised the four-days' dead—not in this is the perfect joy.

"If a Brother Minor knew all languages, all science, and all scripture, if he could prophesy and reveal not only future things, but even the secret of consciences and of souls — not in this consists the perfect joy.

"If he could speak the language of angels, if he knew the courses of the stars and the virtues of plants, if all the treasures of earth were revealed to him, and he knew the qualities of birds, fishes, and all animals, of men, trees, rocks, roots, and waters—not in these is the perfect joy."

"Father, in God's name, I pray you," exclaimed Leo, "tell me in what consists the perfect joy."

"When we arrive at Santa Maria degli Angeli (soaked with rain, frozen with cold, covered with mud, dying of hunger)," said Francis, "and we knock, and the porter comes in a rage, saying 'Who are you?' and we answer, 'We are two of your brethren,' and he says, 'You lie; you are two lewd fellows who go up and down corrupting the world and stealing the alms of the poor. Go away!' and he does not open to us, but leaves us outside in the snow and rain, frozen, starved, all night—then, if thus maltreated and turned away we patiently endure all without murmuring against him; if we think with humility and charity that this porter really knows us truly and that God makes (permits) him to speak to us thus, in this is the perfect joy. Above all the graces and all the gifts which the Holy Spirit gives to His friends is the grace to conquer one's self, and willingly to suffer pain, outrages, disgrace, and evil treatment for the love of Christ."

This sounds very like echoes from the Sermon on the Mount and the epistles and testimonies of Paul. It is a commentary upon Paul's Psalm of Love in the thirteenth chapter of First Corinthians, and on his testimony : " I take pleasure in infirmities, in reproaches, in necessities, in persecutions, in distresses for Christ's sake" (2 Cor. xii. 10).

It is a commentary on the words of Jesus : " A man's life consisteth not in the abundance of the things which he possesseth " (Luke xii. 15), and on those other, often forgotten and neglected words :

Blessed are ye, when men shall revile you, and persecute you, and shall say all manner of evil against you falsely, for My sake. Rejoice, and be exceeding glad (Matt. v. 11, 12).

Francis had found the secret of joy, of power, of purity, and of that enduring influence which still stirs and draws out the hearts of men of faith, of simplicity, of a single eye. Across the centuries he speaks to us in a wooing, compelling message that humbles us at the feet of Jesus in contrition and adoring wonder and love.

He found hidden reservoirs of power in union with Christ ; in following Christ ;

in counting all things loss for Christ; in meekly sharing the labours, the travail, the passion, and the Cross of Christ. Thus his life became creative instead of acquisitive. He became a builder, a fighter, a creator; he found his joy, his fadeless glory, his undying influence, not in possessing things, not in attaining rank and title and worldly pomp and power, but in building the spiritual house, the Kingdom of God—in fighting the battles of the Lord against the embattled hosts of sin and hate and selfishness.

This creative life he found in the way of sacrifice and service. He found his life by losing it. He laid down his life and found it again, found it multiplied a thousandfold, found it being reproduced in myriads of other men.

And this I conceive to be the supreme lesson of the life of Francis for us of The Salvation Army, and for the whole Church of God to-day. For it remains eternally true, it is a law of the Spirit, it is the ever-lasting word of Jesus, that :—

He that findeth his life shall lose it: and he that loseth his life for My sake shall find it (Matt. x. 39).

O Lord! help me, help Thy people everywhere, help the greedy, grasping, stricken world, to learn what mean these words of the Master, and to put them to the test with the deathless, sacrificial ardour of the simple, selfless saint of Assisi!

> I knew that Christ had given me birth
> To brother all the souls of earth,
> And every bird and every beast
> Should share the crumbs broke at the feast.
> *(John Masefield)*.

VII. LOOKING BACKWARD AND FORWARD—AFTER SEVENTY YEARS! *

SEVENTY years are less than a pinpoint in the vastness of God's Eternity, but they are a long, long time in the life of a man. When I was a child a man of seventy seemed to me to be as old as the hills. I stood in awe of him. No words could express how venerable he was. When I looked up to him it was like looking up to the snowy, sun-crowned, storm-swept heights of great mountains.

And now, having lived threescore years and ten, I feel as one who has scaled a mighty mountain, done an exploit, or won a war. What toil it has involved! What dangers have been met and overcome! What dull routine; what thrilling adventure! What love, what joy and sorrow, what defeats and victories, what hopes and fears; what visions and dreams yet to be fulfilled! And the River not far away, yet to be crossed. " My soul, be on thy guard!" I remember and marvel.

* Commissioner Brengle attained his seventieth birthday in 1930.

And yet I feel I am but a child. At times I feel as frisky as a boy and I have stoutly to repress myself to keep from behaving frivolously as a boy, and I hear my friend and brother, mentor and companion of half a century, Paul, saying: " Aged men be sober, grave, temperate " (Titus ii. 2).

Then again I feel as old as I am. The leaden weight of seventy years presses heavily upon me.

I look back and it seems like centuries since I was a care-free little lad ; then some vivid memory will leap up within me, and the seventy years seem like a tale of yesterday and I am again a " wee little boy with the tousled head," playing around the flower-embowered cottage in the tiny village by the little Blue River where I was born.

The average age of man is much less than seventy years, so I am a left-over from a departed generation. But while the snows of seventy winters are on my head, the sunshine of seventy summers is in my heart. The fading, falling leaves of seventy autumns solemnize my soul, but the resurrection life upspringing in flower and tree, the returning song-birds, the laughing, leaping brooks and swelling rivers, and the sweet, soft winds of seventy springtimes gladden me.

A history of the world during the seventy

years would show such an advance socially, politically, educationally, economically, scientifically and morally as has not been seen during any previous thousand years of recorded history. People without a background of knowledge of history may dispute this, but desperate as are the moral, social and economic conditions of great masses of men to-day, those who know the story of the ages will not dispute it.

Woman no longer has to be mistress and plaything of prime ministers and kings to influence the political destinies of nations ; she now sits as man's equal in parliament and senate, proclaims from pulpit and platform the Gospel of God's holiness and redeeming love, and is mistress of her own fortune and person.

Childhood is protected by law. The white slave traffic, while still carried on, is outlawed by civilized nations. Human slavery and serfdom have been swept away among all but the least advanced peoples. Africa has been opened to the light of civilization and the Gospel, and its open sores are being healed. The cannibal islands have been evangelized, and shipwrecked sailors and missionaries are safe on their shore.

When I was a child it took weeks to communicate with Europe, and months to

reach Asia. To-day King George speaks
words of welcome in London to the peace
envoys of nations, and the whole world
" listens in." We in America hear his royal
voice five hours before he spoke, according
to our clocks! Admiral Byrd at the South
Pole speaks, and we hear him over twelve
thousand miles of land and sea before his
voice could reach his companion one
hundred feet away! Time and space are
conquered, and the whole world has become
one vast whispering gallery since I was a
child.

Diseases which had scourged mankind
from time immemorial are now being
banished from the earth. War, as the policy
of nations, is renounced and denounced.
Open diplomacy is an accomplished fact.

Wealth is now looked upon as a trust for
humanity. Instead of fitting out pirate ships
and ravaging the coasts of China as men
would have done long ago, Mr. Rockefeller
gives millions to establish one of the most
beautiful and up-to-date hospitals and medi-
cal schools in the world in Peiping, and
untold millions are cabled across the ocean
to feed the starving peoples.

When I consider the vanishing darkness,
the toppling thrones, the crumbling empires,
the fallen crowns, the outlawed tyrannies,
the mastery of nature's secrets, the harnessing

of her exhaustless energies, the penetration
of all lands with the story and light of the
Gospel, which I have witnessed in my day,
I can but feel that I was born at the beginning of the end of the Dark Ages.

But, while the light increases and widens,
the darkness still comprehends it not. And
while God's "truth is marching on,"
"evil men and seducers" wax worse,
become more and more self-conscious and
class-conscious and organize and mass themselves to fight against God and His Christ
and His saints and soldiers more subtly and
determinedly than at any time since the days
of the Roman persecutions and the Spanish
Inquisition ; and this may result in :

> Vast eddies in the flood
> Of onward time . . .
> And throned races may degrade.

This makes me wish for the strength of
youth that I might share in the battles yet
to be. But that is denied me. I must go on,
like Tennyson's ships, "to the haven under
the hill." But I go on serene in unshaken
confidence that the flood, in spite of all
eddies, flows *onward not backward*, that the
light will evermore increase and that any
triumph of "evil men and seducers" will
be short.

Many of God's children are longing for

Jesus to come in Person, visibly to lead on His hosts to victory. But ever since that wonderful morning forty-five years ago when He baptized me with the Holy Ghost and fire, purifying my heart and revealing Himself within me, I have felt that He meant to win His triumphs through dead men and women—dead to sin, to the world, to its prizes and praises; and all alive to Him, filled with His Spirit, indwelt by His presence, burning with His love, glad with His joy, enduring with His patience, thrilled with His hope, daring with His self-renunciation and courage, being consumed with His zeal; all conquering with His faith, rejoicing in " the fellowship of His sufferings," and gladly made " conformable unto His death." I expect the true Vine to show forth all its strength, its beauty, its fruitfulness *through the branches*.

I do not expect the love of the Father, the eternal intercession of the risen and enthroned Son, the wise and loving and ceaseless ministry of conviction, conversion, regeneration and sanctification of the Holy Ghost, the prayers, and preachings and sacrifice and holy living of the soldiers of Jesus and saints of God, to fail. Jesus is even *now* leading on His hosts to victory, Hallelujah!

I cannot always, if ever, comprehend His

great strategy. My small sector of the vast battlefield may be covered with smoke and thick darkness. The mocking foe may be pressing hard, and comrades may fear and falter and flee, and the enemy may apparently triumph as he did when Jesus died, and when the martyrs perished in sheets of flame, by the sword and headman's axe, mauled by the lion's paw, crunched by the tiger's tooth and slain by the serpent's fang. But the enemy's triumph ever has been and ever will be short, for Jesus is leading on and up, ever on, ever up, never backward, never downward, always forward, ever toward the rising sun. Revivals, resurrection life and power, are resident in our religion. A dead church, a dead Salvation Army corps, may, when we least expect, flame with revival fire, for Jesus, though unseen, is on the battlefield, and He is leading on. " Lo, I am with you alway, even unto the end of the world " (Matt. xxviii. 20).

In the lonely and still night, while others sleep, He stirs some longing soul to sighs and tears and strong cryings and wrestling prayer. He kindles utter, deathless devotion in that soul, a consuming jealousy for God's glory, for the salvation of men, for the coming of the Kingdom of God ; and in that lonely and still night and out of that travail, that agony of spirit, mingled with solemn joy, a revival is born. Behold, " the kingdom of God cometh not with observation " (Luke xvii. 20). There may be no blast of trumpets, no thunder of drums, no flaunting of flags. The revival is born in the heart of some lonely, longing, wrestling, believing, importunate man or woman who will give God no rest, who will not let Him go without He blesses. Bright-eyed, golden-haired, rosy-cheeked dolls can be made by machinery and turned out to order, but living babies are born of sore travail and death agony. So revivals may be simulated, trumped up, made to order, but not so do revivals begotten by the Holy Ghost come.

Three local officers of The Salvation Army were concerned about the spiritual life of their corps. Souls were not being saved. They agreed to spend time in prayer. Saturday night they did not go home. Sunday they were not in the meetings. No one knew where they were. Sunday night there was a great " break " among the sinners and lukewarm Christians. Many souls were at the penitent-form. Many tears were shed. All hearts seemed moved and softened. About ten o'clock at night, with tears streaming down their faces, these three local officers came from under the platform where they had spent Saturday night and all day Sunday in prayer. That was the secret of the great meeting.

Seventy years have passed over my head, fifty-seven of which I have spent in the service of my Lord, and forty-three with The Salvation Army; and the experience and observation of these years confirm me in my conviction that revivals are born, not made, and that God waits to be gracious and aid and answer prayer.

I was converted one Christmas Eve at the age of thirteen, and I have never looked back, though I side-stepped and faltered a bit at times in my early years. Immediately I joined the Church, yielded loyally to its discipline, kept its rules, and though I had not the Blessing of a Clean Heart I felt keenly that I must not prove false or do anything that would bring reproach upon the Church or the cause of Christ. When I was fifteen years old, my mother slipped away to be with the Lord, and I became homeless for the next twelve years, with no one to counsel me; but this loyalty to the rules of the Church safeguarded me.

For five years I taught a Sunday School class, and at the age of twenty-three I became a pastor, with four preaching places on my circuit, in three of which we had blazing revivals. Although not sanctified, I preached all the truth I knew with all my might, and believed what I preached with all my heart, and God blessed me, for He always has blessed and ever will bless such preaching.

When He gloriously sanctified me my knowledge and keen perception of truth were greatly enlarged and quickened, and my preaching became far more searching and effective. And now for forty-seven years God has been giving me revivals with many souls. This has been the glad and consuming ambition of my life. Place, promotion, power, popularity have meant nothing to me as compared with the smile of God and the winning of men to Him. Hallelujah! And this has enabled me to give myself wholly and effectively to my job without thought of what my job would give to me; and I shout *Amen* to my Lord's word: "It is more blessed to give than to receive" (Acts xx. 35).

Many kind and generous things have been said to me and about me, but the greatest compliment ever paid me was by General William Booth, when, on two different occasions, he said to me, "Brengle, you are equal to your job"; a job* to which he appointed me, and in which he took special interest. Since I knew his tongue was not that of an oily flatterer, and that he

* As international evangelist in The Salvation Army.

was not carrying flowers around for pro-
miscuous presentation, I rejoiced ; for one
of my great desires was to gladden his heart,
so often wounded, to put my full strength
so far as possible under his vast burden, and
to ease his anxieties where some others
failed him.

The greatest compliment ever paid to my
work was by Commissioner Hay,* following
my seven months' campaign in Australia.
He wrote the Chief of the Staff, saying
that the campaign not only brought showers
of blessing, but opened up spiritual springs.
Showers are transient in effect, but springs
flow on for ever.

My father-in-law lived to be nearly ninety,
and he said : " As men grow old they
become either sweet or sour." He ripened
sweetly and became more and more gracious
in his old age. I want to be like that.

> Let me grow lovely, growing old,
>   So many fine things do ;
> Laces, and ivory, and gold,
>   And silks need not be new ;
>
> And there is healing in old trees ;
>   Old streets a glamour hold ;
> Why may not I, as well as these,
>   Grow lovely, growing old ?

* Then in charge of Salvation Army work in Australia.

Some painful and a few bitter things may have happened to me during these forty-three years I have been in The Salvation Army, but really I cannot recall them. I refuse to harbour such memories, so they fade away. Why should I pour bitter poison into the sweet wells of my joy, from which I must continue to drink if I would really live? I won't do it. Paul is my patron saint, and he has told me what to do: "Whatsoever things are true, . . . honest, . . . just, . . . pure, . . . lovely, . . . of good report; if there be any virtue, and if there be any praise, think on these things" (Phil. iv. 8). That I will, Paul.

At the same time I do not want to indulge in saccharine sentimentality, for I remember that Jesus said, " Ye are [not the sugar, but] the salt of the earth." I must not lose my saltness.

But too much salt is dangerous, so I must beware. Nor must I ever forget, as our evangelist Paul bids me, to :

Reprove, rebuke, exhort with all long-suffering and doctrine. For the time will come [God forbid that it should come to The Salvation Army!] when they will not endure sound doctrine; but after their own lusts shall they heap to themselves teachers, having itching ears; and they shall turn away their ears from the truth, and shall be turned unto fables (2 Tim. iv. 2–4).

And though retired I must still " watch . . . in all things, endure afflictions, do the work of an evangelist, and make full proof of [my] ministry " (2 Tim. iv. 5). For the solemn day of accounting is yet to come— coming surely, swiftly—when I must render an account of my stewardship ; when the final commendations or condemnations shall be spoken ; when the great prizes and rewards will be given, and the awful de-privations and dooms will be announced.

Apostles though they were, Peter and Paul never lost their awe of that day ; nor must I, for Jesus said :

Many will say to Me in that day, Lord, Lord, have we not prophesied in Thy name ? and in Thy name have cast out devils ? and in Thy name done many wonderful works ? And then will I profess unto them, I never knew you : depart from Me (Matt. vii. 22, 23).

Remembering these words I gird my armour closer, grip my sword, and, watch-ing, praying, marching breast forward, I sing :

My soul, be on thy guard !
  Ten thousand foes arise ;
The hosts of Hell are pressing hard
  To draw thee from the skies.

[119]

The Guest of the Soul

Ne'er think the battle won,
    Nor lay thine armour down :
The fight of faith will not be done
    Till thou obtain the crown !

It is a fight of faith, and faith is nourished
by the word of the Lord, to which I return
daily for my portion and am not denied

Hallelujah !

VIII. TEXTS THAT HAVE BLESSED
ME

WHEN I was a Cadet in The Salvation Army's International Training College, forty-seven years ago, we had on the staff a young officer who had been a wild, reckless sinner. He had been saved but a short while when war broke out in Egypt, and, being a military reservist, he was sent to the front. He had no Bible, and he could remember but one promise—"*My grace is sufficient for thee*" (2 Cor. xii. 9).

In every temptation that assailed, every danger, every hour of spiritual loneliness, it was through this text that he looked up to God and claimed heavenly resources for his earthly needs. And he was not disappointed. His needs were met. God failed him never.

What a happy man to have such a promise! And yet how poor he was ! He was like a beleaguered army with only one line of communication open ; like a city with only one aqueduct for water, or one dynamo for light ; like a room with but one window, or a house with but one door ; like a car with but one cylinder ; like a man with only one lung. There was but one star in his sky.

I remember how poor I felt him to be. He was not a juicy soul. He was not radiant. His face did not shine. It lacked solar light. I rejoiced that he was spiritually alive, but it was such an impoverished life! He was like a diver in the deep sea whose supply of oxygen came down through a pipe line, instead of being like a man on top of the world with all the winds blowing upon him, all the stars twinkling and dancing above him, all the glory of the cloudless days irradiating him.

Now, when I am asked for my favourite promise, I smile. *It is not one text more than another, but* A WHOLE BIBLE that blesses me, assures me, warns and corrects and comforts me. A hundred promises whisper to me. I never know when one of the promises—perhaps one that I have not met for days or even months—may suddenly stand before me, beckon me, speak to me tenderly, comfortingly, authoritatively, austerely; speak to me as though God were speaking to me face to face.

The ancient heroes of the Cross "obtained promises by faith." You can buy a Bible for a few cents or pence, and if you have not the money to buy, a Bible Society will give you one. And the Bible *teems* with promises. They are on almost every page. But your eyes will not see them, your mind will not grasp them, your heart will receive no strength and consolation from them—if you have not faith. The man who goes through the Bible without faith is like the Boers and natives who walked over the diamond fields of Africa all unconscious of the immeasurable wealth beneath their feet.

When I say that I smile at being asked for my favourite promise, and I reply that it is the whole Bible which blesses me, I do not mean that there is no one promise that looms large to me, but rather that there are so many which bless me and meet my daily needs that I am like a man with a home full of sweet children, every one of whom is so dear to him that he cannot tell which he loves most and which is most needful for his happiness.

My spiritual needs are manifold, and there seems to be a promise just suited to my every need, that matches my need as a Yale key matches a Yale lock, as a glove fits the hand, as light answers to my eye and music to my ear, as the flavour of delicious food matches my sense of taste, and as the attar of roses answers my sense of smell ; as the love of one's beloved and the faithfulness of one's friend answer the hunger of the heart.

For three or four years I had known that some day I would have to come to close grips with myself and get the Blessing of a

Clean Heart if I was ever to see God in peace and have the power of the Holy Ghost in my life. At last I began to seek in earnest, and for three or four weeks I had become more and more hungry for the blessing. There were two things confronting me which I felt I could not do, but self had to be crucified. The way of faith was hidden from me because I hesitated to approach it by the way of whole-hearted obedience.

But God was faithful. He did not leave me, but deepened conviction until I was in an agony. At last, at about nine o'clock on Friday morning, January 9th, 1885, I could hold out no longer. My heart broke within me, and I yielded. Then instantly was whispered in my heart this text: "*If we confess our sins, He is faithful and just to forgive us our sins, and to cleanse us from all unrighteousness*" (1 John i. 9). The last part of the text was a revelation to me: "*to cleanse us from all unrighteousness*"—"ALL *unrighteousness.*"

I dropped my head in my hands and said, "Father, I believe that," and instantly peace passing all understanding flooded my soul, and I knew that I was clean. "*The law of the Spirit of life in Christ Jesus*" had "*made me free from the law of sin and death*" (Rom. viii. 2). Hallelujah!

Two days later I preached on the Blessing

and testified to it. But I trembled lest I might lose it. Then the Lord spoke to me in the words of Jesus to Martha, mourning over her dead brother, Lazarus : " *I am the resurrection, and the life : he that believeth in Me, though he were dead, yet shall he live : and whosoever liveth and believeth in Me shall never die* " (John xi. 25, 26).

Again I believed, and in that moment Christ was revealed in me as surely as He was revealed to Paul on the road to Damascus. I melted into tears, and loved my Lord as I never dreamed one could love. Since then I have again and again cried out with Paul : " *I am crucified with Christ : nevertheless I live ; yet not I, but Christ liveth in me : and the life which I now live in the flesh I live by the faith of the Son of God, who loved me, and gave Himself for me* " (Gal. ii. 20). And again and again I have said with Paul : " *What things were gain to me, those I counted loss for Christ. Yea doubtless, and I count all things but loss for the excellency of the knowledge of Christ Jesus my Lord* " (Phil. iii. 7, 8).

When again I feared lest I might fall, these two texts reassured me : " *Fear thou not ; for I am with thee : be not dismayed ; for I am thy God : I will strengthen thee ; yea, I will help thee ; yea, I will uphold thee with the right hand of My righteousness* " (Isa. xli. 10) ; and " *Now unto Him that is able to keep you from falling, and to present you faultless before the presence of His glory with exceeding joy*" (Jude 24).

Then I was tempted with the thought that, when I got old, the light would fade and the fire in my soul would go out. But these texts came with comforting assurance and power to my heart: "*Even to your old age I am He; and even to hoar hairs will I carry you: I have made, and I will bear; even I will carry, and will deliver you*" (Isa. xlvi. 4); and, "*Those that be planted in the house of the Lord shall flourish in the courts of our God. They shall still bring forth fruit in old age; they shall be fat and flourishing*" (Ps. xcii. 13, 14).

I saw that I must not fear, nor be dismayed, in the presence of any trouble or difficulty, but must quietly trust in the Lord. And I must not drift about as so many do, but remain "*planted in the house of the Lord.*"

When I have gone to distant battlefields in far-off lands, among strangers, this promise has put comfort and strength into me: "*My presence shall go with thee, and I will give thee rest*" (Exod. xxxiii. 14). And when I have felt any insufficiency I have been reassured with this promise: "*Who hath made man's mouth? or who maketh the dumb, or deaf, or the seeing, or the blind? have not I the Lord? Now therefore go, and I will be with thy mouth, and teach thee what thou shalt say*" (Exod. iv. 11, 12).

[126]

These are only a few of a multitude of precious promises and words of the Lord which came to me years ago, and which are ever whispering in my mind and heart, challenging my faith, my love, my utter devotion.

They are the joy and rejoicing of my heart; a heritage from the Lord, a lamp to my feet, a light to my path, a sword with which to thrust through the accusations and doubts and fears with which Satan is ever ready to assail me.

Hallelujah !